HYPERACTIVE CHILDREN
A PRACTICAL GUIDE FOR PARENTS

By
Dr Joanne Barton

Registered Charity SCO11849
Established 1985

Published by
The Child & Family Trust, Fleming House, 134 Renfrew Street, Glasgow G3 6ST
Email: publication@cft-scotland.com

Printed by
C & G Print, Troon KA10 6HR

Illustrations and Front Cover by
Ronnie Russell, Troon

ISBN No. 0 9534060 0 8

Foreword

Much has been written about hyperactive children and their families in scientific, pseudo-scientific and entirely fictional books and magazines. Experts have looked for causes in the child, the parents, their genetic endowments or their environments but offer limited help or advice on how to manage the situation.

Dr Joanne Barton and her colleagues have developed a clear and delightfully presented set of straightforward strategies for coming to terms with the disruptive behaviours in the home and community situation. These strategies have evolved from their own clinical experience, are evidence based and have been proven to be effective in a wide range of different social and emotional environments.

There is a great deal still to be learned about the various causes of hyperactive behaviour, the different brain dysfunctions which are associated and the place of pharmacological interventions. In the meantime families need practical and useful advice to help them and to prevent an often fraught situation developing into an unbearable one. This very user-friendly practical guide will be a godsend to many families and their professional advisors.

Professor F. Cockburn

For my mother and father, and Flip, with thanks.

ACKNOWLEDGEMENTS

This book developed out of the work of the Pre-School Overactivity Programme which is a treatment programme for young children affected by hyperactivity disorders. The programme was made possible by the commitment and dedication of a number of people and I would like to thank them here.

The Child and Family Trust supported the Pre-School Overactivity Programme when it was just an idea on paper, and by appointing a Fulton Mackay Nurse to work on the programme, facilitated its development into a working treatment resource. Without the foresight and support of the committee members and trustees of The Child and Family Trust, the programme would never have come into being. My thanks also go to the lady who was the first Fulton Mackay Nurse, Mrs Angela Bower; her calm and balanced approach to the work provided a stabilising influence through the development of the project and its early days. Mrs Janette Lennox has been with us from the start and her insight, as a teacher, into the management of young children with behavioural problems has been invaluable. Ms Suzanne McCrea took over from Mrs Bower as Fulton Mackay Nurse and has brought her own style to the work of the programme; my thanks go to her for that. Dr Seija Sandberg provided considerable support and advice during the development of the project as my supervisor and colleague, for which I am indebted. The illustrations in this book have been produced by Mr Ronnie Russell; his extraordinary talent in sensitively bringing to life the ideas and concepts described in the book is greatly appreciated.

Finally, many thanks must go to Children in Need for their financial assistance in the production of this book and to the long suffering team at C & G Print. They have been patient with me beyond belief. All in all I have been privileged to work with such professional and dedicated people.

Joanne Barton

Glasgow, 1999

The Child and Family TRUST

EASY USE OF THIS BOOK

At first glance you may think there is a lot of reading in this book but look again - and think of it as a handbook that contains important information on how to cope with Hyperactivity disorders in children.

It has:

SECTIONS: The book is split into 14 sections.
Try and follow through each section before going on to the next part.

SUMMARY: At the end of most sections is a summary of important points.

TASKS: These appear directly below the summary on the same page.
The task is designed to enable you to put into practice the contents of that section.
Sometimes there is more than one task, in which case, separate sheets with the appropriate task headed at the top are provided.

WORK SHEETS: Work Sheets are there to be filled in. Although this takes time, you will find them
(Green Sheet)   a helpful guide enabling you to put into action your ideas on each task.

NOTE PAGE: This handbook is for you to record what works and what doesn't.
(Blue Sheet)   In order to do that you have to note these things down.
Use the note pages and refer back to them.

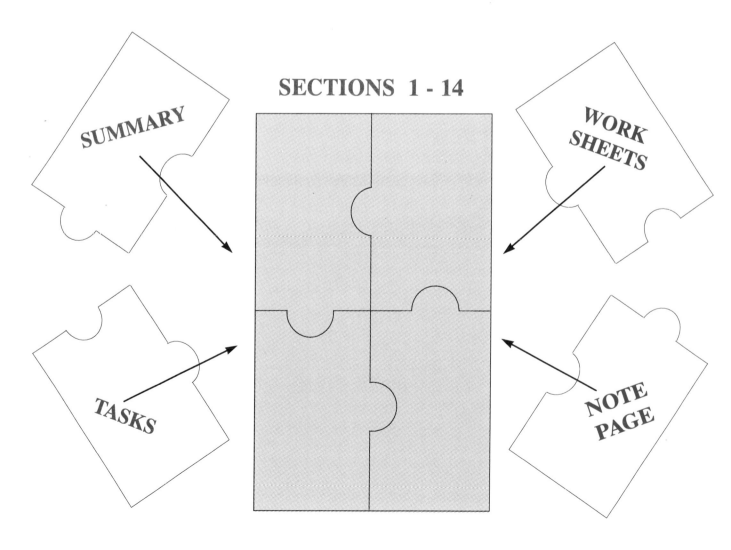

CONTENTS

1. INTRODUCTION

Hyperactivity disorders are amongst the most common behaviour disorders of childhood, affecting up to 5% of school age children. The nature of these disorders is such that they cause considerable disruption to the lives of children who suffer from them and to the lives of their families.

In this book, I have used the term "hyperactivity" to cover a range of behaviour disorders, of varying severity, and to encompass the medically recognised syndromes of Attention Deficit Hyperactivity Disorder and Hyperkinetic Disorder. The main features of hyperactivity disorders are overactivity, impaired attention span and impulsivity. Whilst these are behaviours which all children show at times, hyperactive children show them to a degree which interferes with normal day to day activities, at home, at school and at play. As a result, hyperactive children become unpopular with their families, their peers and their teachers and life can be quite miserable for the child and for those people, primarily their families, who try to help them with their difficulties.

Hyperactivity disorders can be detected at an early stage in a child's life, especially by parents who are often aware that their children are "different". Sadly, it is often not until a child enters primary school and runs into significant difficulties in that setting, that children are referred for professional help. There are distinct advantages in the early identification and treatment of hyperactivity disorders. Early intervention can go some way to relieve the suffering of the child and their family and also prevent the development of other behaviour problems and strained relationships between family members.

Children who suffer from hyperactivity disorders are often referred to Child and Adolescent Psychiatrists for assessment and treatment. In the Department of Child and Adolescent Psychiatry at the Royal Hospital for Sick Children in Glasgow we promoted the early identification and referral of children with such disorders. Traditionally we worked with families on an individual basis.

However, we were aware from practical experience and from research, that people often get more out of working as part of a group and that they prefer to do it this way rather than working on their own. If you put a group of people together, who all have experience of the same problem and are working towards a common goal, they will support each other in achieving that goal. This is the basis of slimming groups and other self help groups. Because of this, we decided that instead of treating children and their families individually, we would see them in groups. We developed an intervention programme for pre-school age children with hyperactivity disorders. The programme consisted of a parent training group and a behaviour therapy group for the children. We called this treatment programme the Pre-School Overactivity Programme. Once we had developed our ideas for the Programme we were faced with the task of getting the groups up and running. We were supported, in this by The Child and Family Trust who funded a Fulton Mackay Nurse to work on the programme for a period of three years. The Programme is now part of the service offered by the Hyperkinetic Team at The Royal Hospital for Sick Children.

This book was originally produced as a handbook to accompany the treatment programme. Its purpose was to provide a resource for the parents taking part in the programme, to remind them of the theoretical and practical aspects of the work covered in the treatment sessions and to give them something to refer to when the programme was over. The book provides useful information for anyone with a child with such difficulties and so it was decided that, with some modification, it should be published. The Child and Family Trust have, once again, been instrumental in this by supporting the publication of the book as part of their philosophy of helping children and their families, where the child is affected by illness or suffers for some other reason.

The book provides an overview of hyperactivity disorders, what is known about their causation and presentation. In addition, it attempts to portray a child's viewpoint by discussing why children

5

behave in certain ways. It introduces ideas about effective ways of communicating with children and respecting them as individuals. These are important foundation stones which must be in place before the more complex behaviour management techniques described in the later chapters of the book can be attempted. The book, therefore, should be worked through chapter by chapter.

Although the Pre-school Overactivity Programme was developed for young children, the techniques described in this book can be applied, with appropriate adjustment, to children of any age. They are designed to promote positive behaviour by helping children develop more effective control over their own behaviour. Behavioural control is something which every child has to learn. Small children are entirely dependent on adults to control and direct their behaviour. As they get older they learn to do this for themselves. Children with hyperactivity disorders take longer to develop behavioural control and they have to work harder at it and need more help in achieving control from the adults who care for them.

The strategies described in the book are not new. Parent behaviour management training and child cognitive behaviour therapies have been used and researched extensively in the treatment of a variety of childhood behavioural problems. The techniques described have been drawn from tried and tested behaviour management programmes; in particular, the ideas and techniques of Carolyn Webster Stratton (1) and those of Dinkmeyer and McKay described in the STEP programme (2) have been adjusted and applied to the behavioural difficulties of children with hyperactivity disorders.

The purpose of the behaviour management strategies described in this book is to promote more appropriate patterns of behaviour in children whose own behavioural control is immature. It often takes a while to establish new patterns of behaviour and the course in achieving this is often up and down, with two steps forwards and one step back or one step forwards and two back. Things often get worse before they get better. It is, in fact, a good sign if a child's behaviour deteriorates when new behaviour management strategies are introduced. It means things have changed. Children often do not like change, particularly if it means that they do not get their own way. They will try to resist the change and this resistance is reflected in a deterioration in their behaviour. It is important not to give up at this point, to recognise this as progress and to keep going with increased resolve.

Doing this sort of work is very hard, emotionally and physically, and it is particularly hard when you are already tired and exhausted. It is important to find the energy from somewhere. It is better to do the work now than wait; it will be harder the longer you wait. By doing the work now, you will not only make life better for your child and yourself right now, but you may also help prevent further problems from developing later on when your child is older. It is important however, to recognise your own exhaustion and to find ways to relieve this. You have to look after yourself in order to care for your child properly and so you must take time to see to your own needs.

Consistency is very important in behaviour management and so it is essential that you discuss the changes you are going to make with the people who help you look after your child. Let them read the book as well; people like grandparents, aunts and uncles and those who regularly help to look after your child. Tell them about it, let them read over the book and discuss it with them. At various stages in the book there is a task for you to do which has been designed to help you practice the techniques described in the preceding chapter. It is important that you do these tasks with your partner and talk to each other about what you have done, check each others work and comment on what you think you have done well and not so well. Consistency between grown-ups is vital for success.

The material covered in this book will provide a base from which to work in the future. Once you have finished the book, you will have to carry on with everything you have learned. The book will suggest to you a new way of thinking about your children and their hyperactivity and new ways of managing their behaviour so that, with your help, they can overcome some of the problems they have now and achieve their potential.

1. Webster Stratton C. (1989) The Parents and Children Series. Castalia Publishing Co. Minnesota.
2. Dinkmeyer and McKay, Systematic Training for Effective Parenting. The Parents Handbook. American Guidance Service Circle Pines Minnesota 55014.

2. WHAT IS HYPERACTIVITY?

Hyperactivity is not a new phenomenon. It has been recognised for many years and has been, and continues to be, the subject of extensive research and investigation. The first good descriptions of hyperactivity appeared in medical literature in the early 1900's when Professor George Still described children who were suffering from what he called "morbid defects of moral control". Professor Still believed that children who were overactive and impulsive were biologically pre-disposed to this sort of behaviour (that is, their genetic make-up put them at risk of being hyperactive) and that the environment in which they lived could either make their behaviour worse or better, depending on the quality of their housing, their education and so on.

Following the first world war there was an epidemic of encephalitis (inflammation of the brain). Many of the children who recovered from this illness presented with restless, overactive behaviour and had difficulty concentrating. In fact their behaviour was very similar to that of children suffering from hyperactivity disorders. This led people to think that hyperactivity disorders might be the result of some form of brain damage and the disorder became known, for a while, as Minimal Brain Damage Syndrome. Thus, for a long time it was thought that children who suffered from hyperactivity were in fact suffering from brain damage. However, in most cases there was no evidence to support this when the children were examined.

Researchers continued to investigate the possible causes of hyperactivity and great advances were made in the 1930's when it was discovered that a group of drugs known as neuro-stimulants were effective in treating the disorder. Currently there is considerable evidence to support the role of genetics in causing hyperactivity. Brain scans looking at both the structure of the brain (its size and shape) and its function (how it works) and electro-encephalography (the study of the electrical activity of the brain) show that the brains of children with hyperactivity work differently from children who are not hyperactive. What these differences mean is not yet clear. Further research is needed to determine whether these differences reflect a causative process or whether they are the result of the effect of hyperactivity on brain development.

Children are affected by hyperactivity to different degrees. Some children are very mildly affected such that their behaviour is only slightly different from that of an unaffected child and these children suffer little interference in their day to day lives. At the other end of the spectrum are those children with very severe disorders who suffer serious disturbance in all areas of their life. In this book we are going to use the term **"hyperactivity"** to cover everything from mild to severe problems.

Hyperactivity is in some cases a persistent problem. Some children appear to grow out of the disorder when they get older, however, for others, the disorder continues throughout childhood and into adolescence and adulthood. Children who suffer from hyperactivity require help from the adults who look after them, to manage their disorder for them everyday, until they have learned to manage it for themselves.

Hyperactivity disorders are more common in boys than in girls. The reasons for this are not clear. For simplicity and the sake of space, I will refer to he or him throughout the book, but what is being said can equally be applied to boys and girls.

The three main features of Hyperactivity are:

Inattention - difficulty concentrating

Excessive activity - being on the go all the time

Impulsivity - not thinking things through before acting and not being able to wait for things.

Let us look at the three components of hyperactivity in more detail..

INATTENTION

Children who are hyperactive have great difficulty concentrating on any one thing for any length of time, compared to children of the same age. It becomes even more difficult if they are being asked to concentrate on something which they find boring in the first place. They can concentrate better on things which they enjoy or are interested in (just like anyone else!). Concentrating is quite complicated and quite a hard thing to do. You have to be able to start whatever it is you want to do, then you have to keep going with it for a while and at the same time, not be put off or distracted by something else which is going on near by. Not surprising then that it is so hard!

EXCESSIVE ACTIVITY

Hyperactive children are on the go all the time. Most children run for a reason, for example when they are playing "chase" or running after a ball or a toy car. Hyperactive children run for the sake of it, they run about all the time and even when they are sitting down they fidget. Some children are even very restless when they are asleep.

IMPULSIVITY

Hyperactive children seem to do things without thinking through the consequences of their actions. They may know what the rules are but, even so, they can't seem to stop themselves doing something that they want to, even though they know it will get them into trouble later. They seem to have very little self control and to be afraid of nothing! In addition they don't seem to learn from their mistakes so that although you have told them a hundred times not to do something they still go ahead and do it and get in a mess as a result. This kind of behaviour can make people think that hyperactive children are being deliberately disobedient. Whilst, like all children, they will be disobedient at times, it is important to remember that hyperactive children do have problems thinking through the consequences of their actions.

Impulsivity shows itself in other ways; in particular, in difficulty waiting for things. Hyperactive children find it hard to wait for things they want such as their turn in a game, or rewards. If you give a child the choice of having a biscuit now or waiting five minutes and then getting two, most children will choose to wait. Hyperactive children on the other hand will opt for having a biscuit **now.**

These three core problems (Inattention, Excessive Activity, Impulsivity) can cause havoc with the child's relationship with his family, teachers, classmates and in fact, with the whole world! A further difficulty results from the fact that hyperactivity is unpredictable. Sometimes your child will seem to be able to hold it all together and behave; and at other times, he is all over the place! This is frustrating for you as a parent but imagine what it is like for him! Relationships become strained because you never know what he is going to do next.

The three core behaviours described above are not in themselves abnormal. All children (and some of us as adults) show these behaviours at times. All children will at times be overactive, or not able to concentrate or think things through before acting. Children with hyperactivity disorders however, show these behaviours to an extent which causes them problems in their day to day lives. Hyperactive children do these things more often and in a more extreme way!

WHAT CAUSES HYPERACTIVITY?

Unfortunately there is no easy answer to this question. Hyperactivity is not like many of the illnesses of childhood such as coughs and colds or throat infections where we can say that the problem is caused by a bug or a virus. We do not know exactly what causes children to be hyperactive. A great deal of research has been and continues to be done, in this area. In this section of the book I will go over some of the things which research has shown to be involved in causing hyperactivity.

First of all it is important to say that hyperactivity can occur as part of another illness. A child who is suffering from another problem may show signs of being hyperactive because of that problem. Children's brains are quite vulnerable and can be damaged by various things at various stages in the child's development, even during the time they are growing and developing in the womb. Thus brain development may be affected by a mother suffering from a viral infection whilst she is pregnant or if a mother abuses drugs or alcohol during her pregnancy. A child's brain may also be affected by infection or injury after they are born. Children who have suffered brain damage at some stage in their lives as a result of brain infections (meningitis, encephalitis) or accidents are more likely to show hyperactive behaviour. Children who have suffered from lead poisoning (this is not so common these days) are also more likely to be hyperactive, as are children who suffer from learning disability for whatever reason. Other medical problems can, in the short term, make children behave in a hyperactive way. Also some medication used to treat illnesses will make a child hyperactive whilst they are taking the medication.

You will probably have read or heard something about hyperactivity being caused by food. There

has been a great deal of publicity about food allergies, particularly allergies to food additives (things like colourings and preservatives) causing hyperactivity. This has been investigated in great detail by researchers and the results have shown that food does not in general cause hyperactivity and so, in most cases, we cannot treat hyperactivity by putting children on special diets. You might have tried putting your child on a diet and in most cases it will not have made any difference. However, in some cases children are allergic to certain foods or food additives and eating these things causes them to behave in a hyperactive way. The sensible thing to do in such cases is simply to avoid those foods which make the child's behaviour worse. Seeking the advice of a specialist in nutrition is important if you are considering putting your child on a diet as a way of managing their hyperactivity.

In the majority of cases, there are no obvious causes for the hyperactivity, as described above. In such cases, it is likely that a number of different factors are involved in causing a child to be hyperactive. Research has shown that hyperactivity runs in families. Studies have been done which have looked at relatives of hyperactive children and they have found that a hyperactive child is four times more likely to have someone in their family who has the same problem. Other studies have confirmed this and have shown that it is not just to do with families living together and thus showing similar types of behaviour, but in fact something is passed on from one generation to the next; that is to say, hyperactivity is inherited. At this point in time we do not know what is inherited or how it is inherited. Researchers are however beginning to look at the role of different genes in the causation of hyperactivity.

Another area which is attracting a lot of interest in understanding what causes hyperactivity is the structure and function of the brain. We can now, with modern technology, (Computerised Tomography and Magnetic Resonance Imaging) look at how the brain works and also look for differences in the way the brains of people with particular disorders work. Whilst the studies which have been done on hyperactive children are few in number, because they are technically difficult to do, they have shown that in some hyperactive children, there are subtle differences in brain structure and function. We also know that certain drugs which alter brain chemistry (our brains require a large range of different chemicals which are produced naturally in our bodies, in order to function properly) are effective in treating hyperactivity in children. This might suggest that the brain chemistry of children with these disorders is slightly different in some way. However, the precise nature of these differences is not known at this time. Neither is it known whether these differences in brain structure and function, which are only small differences, are causative, or if they represent the effect of the child's different behaviour on brain development. Considerably more research is needed to answer these questions.

Children and even very young babies have their own particular temperamental style right from the word go. As a parent you will know this. Very often we find that hyperactive children have been difficult when they were very small or from early on in life. Often there have been problems with sleeping and eating and they have been difficult children to comfort. Temperament affects how your child responds to you and this in turn will affect how you respond to your child. It is important to remember that relationships and interactions with others are two-way things.

Children with an easy temperament, (that is children who are relaxed, sleep and eat well and don't cry very much) are easy to respond to in a positive way because they make you feel good about yourself and reassure you that you are a good parent. Because you feel good about yourself as a parent, you will be relaxed and confident with your child. This in turn will make the child feel good. On the other hand, difficult children, who cry a lot and don't eat or sleep very well, make you feel you are a hopeless parent, that you can't get anything right for them. You feel demoralised and respond to your child, who is making you feel this way, in a very negative fashion. The child will sense that you do not like him very much and this in turn will make him feel bad about himself. From this we can see that interaction and relationships with children are important in terms of their effect on a child's behaviour. If you have a child who is temperamentally difficult it is very easy to get into a negative style of interacting with him. This in turn will cause him to feel bad about himself and may

lead to a deterioration in his behaviour. Thus, whilst parents don't cause children to be hyperactive, the way they respond to a hyperactive child can make things worse.

We must also consider the effect of environment on a child's behaviour and whilst it is unlikely that a child's environment (that is where they live and their community) will cause them to be hyperactive, environmental factors can be important in either making their behaviour worse or better. A child who is living in an ideal environment with adequate housing and schooling, may cope reasonably well even though he is hyperactive. On the other hand, a child living in conditions of deprivation, in an overcrowded house and attending a school with large classes, may not survive so well if he is hyperactive.

In summary, it is likely that hyperactivity is caused by a number of factors and that genetics, brain structure and function are all subtly involved. Hyperactivity is not caused by bad parenting, but the way parents and adults respond to children does affect the way a child behaves.

DO HYPERACTIVE CHILDREN SUFFER FROM OTHER THINGS AS WELL?

Hyperactivity is associated with a number of other problems including oppositional defiant disorder, conduct disorder, specific learning difficulties and speech and language disorders. In addition, some hyperactive children also develop anxiety and depression. Approximately 50% of hyperactive children will have some form of additional problem which will require treatment in its own right. Because of this, the assessment and treatment of hyperactive children should be undertaken by specialists with experience in managing children with these disorders.

CAN HYPERACTIVITY BE TREATED?

Hyperactivity can be treated, and the aim of treatment is to reduce symptoms so that the child suffers as little disruption to his day-to-day life as possible. There are a number of different treatments for hyperactivity which can be considered under two headings, drug treatment and other treatments.

Drug treatment

There are drugs which are effective in treating children who suffer from hyperactivity. The drugs used most commonly are amphetamine-like drugs (such as Methylphenidate [Ritalin] and Dexamphetamine [Dexedrine] but some antidepressants are also useful [Imipramine]). As with most drugs, these medications have side effects and so the decision to prescribe medication requires careful consideration, balancing the potential benefits of using the drug against the known side effects. Medication is rarely used in pre-school age children, largely because its use is relatively under-explored in this age group.

Other treatments

Other treatments which are important, either on their own or in combination with medication, for the treatment of hyperactivity and associated problems are cognitive and behaviour therapies. These treatments aim to teach and train children how to control their behaviour. We all have to learn how to behave and hyperactive children are no different in this respect. When we are very young, our parents control our behaviour for us. As we get older we begin to do this for ourselves by following the example of our parents, teachers and our friends and responding to what these people tell us to do. For most of us this happens naturally and without too much of a struggle, for hyperactive children it takes longer and they have to work much harder to get it right.

Cognitive and behaviour therapies use this principle, that children learn about behaviour control from others, by using various strategies to intensify this learning process. In the case of young children, we, as professionals, rely on parents to help their children learn and to do the teaching. Parents spend more time with their child than anyone else and so are in the best position to help. When children are older we can hand them some of the responsibility for doing this work and we work with them directly in behaviour management.

As a parent you will already be using a variety of behaviour management strategies naturally as part of your day to day interaction with your child - all parents do. The material covered in this book will provide you with a training in additional, more specific behaviour management techniques. The techniques you will learn about will become second nature so that eventually you won't think about using them. The idea is that you develop a new way of looking after your child. In addition, as your child sees and experiences you using these techniques, he will learn to do these things for himself. You will have shown him how to manage his own behaviour. You will learn ways of dealing with your child's behaviour which will encourage him to behave in a different way and at the same time help him to feel good about himself. As a result of this, life becomes more fun. You can enjoy your child and spending time with him is really good instead of being a continuous battle.

WHAT ABOUT THE FUTURE?

In some cases hyperactivity and the problems associated with it can continue throughout a person's life. The problem which usually arises first is that of difficulties in school. Hyperactive children often run into problems in the school setting.

Because hyperactive children find it hard to concentrate, especially on boring things, school work is often very difficult for them. They find it extremely hard to do their lessons in class and are very easily distracted by other things going on round about them. They lose concentration on their lessons and instead get up and run around the classroom or go and talk to someone else. Because of this they get into trouble with the teacher for disrupting the class. Also they can fall quite a long way behind in their work. You can imagine that if we don't do something about this and they carry on in this way throughout their school career, they can miss-out on a lot of their education. This in turn may affect their job opportunities once they have left school.

At the same time in school, hyperactive children sometimes find it hard to make friends. Other children are put off by the fact that the hyperactive child won't wait their turn in games or always seems to want to do things their way. This can lead to children falling out and having fights. Also their behaviour in the classroom, of not getting on with their work and disrupting other people makes them unpopular. The hyperactive child knows that he is unpopular and this affects his self esteem. He will lose confidence about making friends and he may become quite isolated and lonely. These problems in relationships with other people can last throughout life.

The problem of overactivity lessens as children get older so that in adolescence and adulthood it is much less of a problem. Academic under-achievement and difficulties with relationships are the areas in which hyperactive children run into most problems in later life. By acting now to do something to help your child, hopefully you will be able to prevent some of these difficulties.

PARENT CHILD RELATIONSHIPS

Being a parent is not an easy task and it is even harder when your child has a problem. As adults we tend to have ideas about how children should behave. When they don't behave this leads to parents feeling badly about themselves and towards their child. It is then most likely that interaction between parent and child will deteriorate; this in turn will have a long lasting effect on the child. Parents of hyperactive children are at risk of becoming very critical, controlling and directive, because of the way their child behaves.

It is most likely that you have been coping with your child's hyperactivity for a long time and you are probably exhausted. It is important to remember that the way you behave affects your child just as the way he behaves affects you. His disruptive behaviour irritates and exhausts you, but your response to his behaviour will affect him. It is important to stop and think about what you are doing and how it will seem to your child, so that you can make the best use of a situation or incident to help your child learn from it.

If a child does something nice or achieves something we praise and reward them. This is known as positive feedback or interaction. When a child does something which we don't like we try to stop this and may end up having to use some sort of punishment or sanction. This is negative feedback or interaction.

Hyperactive children spend so much of their time doing things that you don't want them to do that you in turn spend most of your time "punishing" them for it. The world becomes a very negative place for hyperactive children. Most of the interaction they have with their parents, teachers and friends is negative. This in turn has an effect on their **self esteem.** They feel that they get it wrong all the time and that people don't like them

much because of it. They think badly of themselves and don't like themselves very much. It may seem that these are rather sophisticated ideas for a young child; they may not be able to put it into words but this is what they are feel. Hyperactive children may experience years of negative interaction, being unable to meet the demands of family, teachers and friends. It is our job as professionals and yours as parents to see that this does not happen.

Much of the work covered in this book is about your relationship with your child. You have a child who is hyperactive and who at times is very difficult to look after. You will sometimes interact with your child in a negative way and you are quite tired and fed up with it all. The aim of the work outlined in this book is to turn things around so that you and your child can interact with each other in a positive way. It will be so much nicer for him and without doubt you will feel better too!

SUMMARY

◆ The core features of hyperactivity disorders are overactivity, inattention and impulsivity. In addition, many hyperactive children are also defiant and cheeky and sometimes aggressive.

◆ All children show these behaviours to some extent, but hyperactive children show them to a greater degree and more often than would usually be expected.

◆ Up to 5% of school age children have problems with hyperactivity.

◆ Boys are more often affected than girls, but boys and girls who have hyperactivity have the same sorts of problems.

◆ Parents do not cause hyperactivity but the way they behave may, in turn, affect the way their child behaves.

◆ Hyperactive children are at risk of receiving a lot of negative interaction from their parents, teachers and friends. This can make them feel bad about themselves and this in turn affects the way they behave.

◆ Hyperactivity can continue to cause problems for children as they get older, even when they are adults so it is important to treat them when they are young to prevent or minimise any difficulties in later life.

TASK

A great deal of the work you are going to do over the course of this book will involve looking in close detail at what your child does and also what you do in response to your child. This might seem quite strange and so to get you used to it we are going to start with a simple task which involves you in observing your child's and your own behaviour and how this makes you feel.

Over the next week, try to find three occasions on which you and your child enjoy doing something together and record them on the work sheet on the next page. It is important that both you and your child enjoy the activity.

WORKSHEET:

Record on this sheet the three occasions on which you and your child did something together which you both enjoyed. Under the heading, **ACTIVITY**, record what you did together and how you knew your child was enjoying himself.

DATE   **ACTIVITY**

1.

2.

3.

3. UNDERSTANDING CHILDREN'S BEHAVIOUR

If we are to try to help children with their behavioural problems it is important that we spend some time to begin with, trying to understand why they behave the way they do. All sorts of different reasons are used to explain why children misbehave including the idea that a child is going through a "stage" such as the "terrible twos". People also say things like "boys will be boys". Children misbehave in different ways at different times for a variety of reasons. They are a bit like adults that way. Sometimes children will misbehave to get attention or to get their own back on someone. In the case of children who are hyperactive, sometimes they misbehave because they haven't thought through the consequences of their actions. Whatever the reason for the misbehaviour it is important that you remember that you can do something to help your child with their behaviour. To do this it is important to take some time to try to understand children's behaviour and misbehaviour. In this Chapter we will talk about why children misbehave.

MISBEHAVIOUR

As mentioned above, children misbehave for a variety of reasons, as a way of getting attention, as a way of trying to control a situation, as a way of getting their own back for something and because they feel that they can't do anything right anyway. Hyperactive children misbehave because they are overactive and impulsive in addition to the reasons mentioned before. When children misbehave they will often realise that they have done something wrong and become upset about this. They will be worried about the fact they have got in a mess and made you angry. Although it may not seem that way to you, when your child misbehaves he will usually feel pretty bad about it.

It is important that you are able to recognise what sort of behaviour you are dealing with before you start to try to solve the problem. Trying to understand why your child is misbehaving will give you some ideas about what to do to stop the misbehaviour. Take some time to think about what he is doing and what is happening as a result of his behaviour. In particular you should think about how the behaviour is making you feel.

Attention seeking behaviour

All children want attention. Usually, they prefer to get positive attention - a smile, an encouraging remark, a hug. If they don't get it that way, however, they will try anything. This usually means resorting to misbehaviour which very quickly gets attention from adults - albeit negative attention.

Children prefer to get negative attention rather than nothing at all.

Attention seeking behaviour is changed by our changing the way we respond to it. This is achieved by showing a child that he can get attention for positive behaviour, but negative behaviour will be ignored. To do this we must focus on constructive or positive behaviour and ignore misbehaviour. Remember that responding to misbehaviour even by getting angry with the child is giving him attention and that by giving attention in this way, we are in fact reinforcing the behaviour and making it more likely that it will happen again.

ANYTHING ELSE .. OH MASTER!!

We must ignore misbehaviour and give attention to positive behaviour in ways that children are not expecting. The emphasis must be taken away from **"getting"** attention and placed on **"giving"** attention. Attention is something which you give to your child when you want to, not when he demands it of you. This does mean, however, that you have to work very hard to tune into your child's positive behaviour, don't miss any opportunity to reward him with praise for positive behaviour, no matter how small. You will be very used to responding to your child when he has done something wrong and you will very likely switch off from him when he is doing something positive - being quiet, watching television etc. These are just the times when you need to pay him some attention, tell him how well he is doing and how much you like his behaviour. So the best way of giving attention is when your child is least expecting it, not when he has misbehaved!

Control

In general, children need to know who is in control, who is responsible for looking after them and whether or not they are capable of that responsibility. Small children respond well to clearly defined rules and limits. They like to know what is acceptable and what is not as this gives them a sense of security. Children rely on adults to provide containing limits. In situations where children are not sure of what the limits or rules are, they will behave in such a way as to test the limits and rules, to see how far they have to go before a limit is put in place. In other words, they misbehave until someone controls their behaviour for them. As children get older, it is a good idea to involve them in negotiating the limits and rules, to help them learn to set their own limits. Hyperactive children find limits hard, but nevertheless need them.

When you are faced with a situation in which a child is challenging the rules, it is important to remember you are the adult in such situations and therefore control lies with **YOU** not your child. Have this in mind and then manage the situation from there. Small children are not capable of controlling situations. If they are allowed to get into a position of control, they often get quite frightened, feeling that they are out of their depth and there is no one to help them. Often their behaviour deteriorates further when they feel this way, so it is an important first step that you let your child know that you are in control and whatever he does you can manage and cope with his behaviour, even if you don't feel that way!

Angry children

Children get cross with their parents and grown-ups for various reasons. For example they may have been denied something they wanted or they have been prevented from doing something they wanted to do. When a child is angry about something they may show their upset by saying something hurtful or doing something which they think will cause upset. In these situations it is important to remember that, in fact, the child is feeling pretty bad. Although you may feel like retaliating, it is important that you don't do this. You must remain calm and show that you understand what your child is feeling and that you still care about him. If your child tells you that he hates you, tell him you understand that he is angry with you and that you still love him. Try to ignore the misbehaviour, distract your child onto something positive and reward that behaviour. Give your child praise as soon as you can.

Low self-esteem

Children who have poor self-esteem often misbehave. They have no confidence in their ability to succeed and so they give up trying to do things well. Instead, they may try to prove how awful they are by misbehaving. It is as though they are trying to show us how bad they think they are and to convince us that they are useless. Children with low self-esteem sometimes don't seem to respond to anything their parents try to do to help them. This in turn makes the parents feel as though they are useless.

Hyperactive children are particularly at risk of developing low self-esteem because their behaviour so often gets them into trouble. They get used to being in trouble, to being told off and told that they are bad and so they begin to believe this about themselves and behave accordingly.

To help children who have poor self-esteem it is important to focus on their strengths and the things they do well. Praise and reward all their efforts and ignore as much of their misbehaviour as possible.

Hyperactive behaviour

As the parent of a hyperactive child you will know only too well that their behaviour frequently gets them into trouble. They rush into things without thinking of the consequences and because they do everything in such a hurry, things often get broken or spoiled. Later on in the book we will discuss ways of helping your child in specific situations but in general there are a few basic principles to have in mind when trying to help hyperactive children.

Firstly you will have to try to think ahead for your child and anticipate where problems might arise and plan for these. Think about what you and your child have to do each day and plan activities with his difficulties in mind. Explain to him what he will be expected to do in each situation and suggest how he might like to go about doing those things. When you are simply going to be at home (not so simple really!) remember to try to keep him busy. If he is occupied doing something he enjoys, he will be less likely to get into trouble. You have to resign yourself to the fact that you probably won't be able to leave him to his own devices, so try to plan what you have to do in such a way that you can keep your eye on your child or better still, involve him in what you have to do. Make sure you have something he can do all the time, but be careful to think about how it will seem from his point of view. Remember that the things that adults enjoy doing may not be what children like!

From what has been described above you can see that **we can help children change their behaviour by changing the way that we respond to them.** We don't make children misbehave, but the way we respond might keep the "bad" or misbehaviour going. The way we as grown-ups manage a child's behaviour will (or will not) help them learn how to manage their own behaviour. Think about how you want your child to behave and then try and behave that way yourself first of all.

We all have to learn how to behave. As small children our parents managed our behaviour for us. As we got older, we started to do this for ourselves; adults helped us with this by telling us what to do and we also copied what other people did, especially our parents, teachers and friends. Most of us learned the rules of behaviour quickly and easily. It is more difficult for hyperactive children who have to work harder to control their behaviour.

So you have a huge responsibility to your child to help him learn how to control his behaviour. Later on in this book we are going to describe behaviour management strategies for you to use to try to help your child. In order for you to succeed in using these techniques you need to put in time and effort in order to **build a positive relationship with your child.** This will be the foundation stone for the work you are going to do with him. To build a positive relationship with your child you must show him that you **respect him.** If you expect your child to respect you, you have to start from a position of respecting him. Take a few moments to consider what you think about your child. What sort of person is he and how would you describe him to someone who doesn't know him?

How much of what you thought of just then was critical ("he's a nightmare", "he's the devil in disguise")? Think about what your usual day is like with your child. How much of your time do you spend yelling and shouting at him and telling him about all the things he has done wrong? Quite a lot I would think - and for good reasons. His behaviour is very difficult. But if you are going to turn things around for your child, you have to first change the way you think about him. Start to think about all his good qualities ("he is such a loving child", "he can be really kind"). Start to respect your child as an individual, respect him in the way you would like him to respect you. From here you can start to build a positive relationship with your child which will allow you to help him with his behaviour problems.

It is also very important to your relationship with your child that you **take time to have fun.** It is hard to find time when you are busy but it doesn't need to be very long. It is the quality of the time not the amount of time you spend with your child that matters. Try to set aside some time each day which is just for you and your child to enjoy yourselves. You must choose something that you both enjoy doing. That way neither of you will feel as though you are being forced to do something. **If you have more than one child you must spend time with each child in turn and they and you must respect each others time.**

MAKE TIME FOR ALL YOUR CHILDREN
... READING BEDTIME STORIES.

Encourage your child as much as you can. Your child must feel that you believe in him if he is to believe in himself. Children need to have at least one important person who loves them. Show your child that you love him by what you say and do.

Being a parent is very hard and getting it right is extremely difficult. No one gets it right all of the time. One of the really difficult things is knowing when to let your child make decisions for himself even though he might make the wrong decision and get in a mess. Sometimes parents become overprotective and try to do everything for their children in an attempt to protect them from getting things wrong. Parents of hyperactive children are particularly at risk of doing this. Hyperactive children frequently get in a mess because of their inattentive, hyperactive behaviour. As a result their parents often try to take over and do everything for

them so that this doesn't happen. This saves the mess but it gives a message to the child which says that he cannot do even simple things. Being on the back of your child constantly, e.g. **stop that, don't do that! let me do that! you don't do it like that!** undermines a child's self confidence. Doing everything for a child robs him of opportunities to learn. It may take longer to do and not be as neat and tidy as you could do it, if you allow your child to do things for himself, but imagine how pleased he will feel when he has managed to do it by himself.

So, don't try to do everything for your child, let him have a go at things. You can make some suggestions about how he might like to go about doing things but let him try for himself. By doing this you will help him develop his self-esteem and self-confidence.

4. UNDERSTANDING PLAY

Play is probably the most important thing that your children do. By playing, children learn about themselves and the world about them, how things work and how people feel about things. Play is vital to a child's development. Through play, children develop physical, intellectual, social and emotional skills. Adults often overlook the importance of play and dismiss it as something children do to occupy their time but which serves no useful purpose. We also make the mistake of believing that children know how to play. If you give a child a toy, they will play with it to an extent, but they will get so much more out of the activity if an adult plays with them and helps them learn how to play. They need someone to show them what to do and the best people to do this are their parents. Different types of play will help children with the development of particular skills. In addition, play is a useful tool which we can use to help children with their behaviour. As therapists working with children with behaviour problems, most of the treatment and therapy we do involves play. We use different games and techniques to help children learn about their behaviour and how to control it.

Many adults have forgotten how to play and some will not have been played with when they were children and so never really learned what it was all about. Adults often feel silly and embarrassed about playing with their children. Instead they feel that it is their job to see that the child has toys to play with and that they come to no harm. Sometimes adults feel that they must control play so that, for example, the child builds the house the right way or dresses the doll properly. Some adults also compete with children during play. The next section of the book describes different kinds of play and how to play with a child.

One of the first things that babies and children start to do is to examine and handle toys. How often do you see babies putting things into their mouths and gazing at rattles or passing a toy from one hand to the other? This **LOOKING AND HANDLING PLAY** is how children find out how things work and learn about colour and texture. The child is finding out about the toy, what it feels like, what sort of noises it makes. Sometimes children will take things to pieces to find out how they work. You can give small children specific toys to feel and play with in this way.

As children get older and get more interested in taking things apart, find toys which can be taken to bits and put back together again.

Sometimes children will take toys apart which are not supposed to be taken apart and toys will get broken. Hyperactive children can be very destructive in this way because they don't stop to think that they might not be able to put the toy back together. Sometimes you can help a child put things back together and sometimes you can stop your child before he takes the toy to bits and help him examine the toy without breaking it. It is easy to lose your temper when a child has apparently destroyed a new toy. You can, however, use this as learning experience. Help your child understand that by taking the toy apart he has broken it. This way you can help children learn to take care of things and think before they try to take things to bits.

Once children become mobile they will start to engage in **ACTIVE PLAY** such as running, jumping, balancing, reaching, stretching, skipping and hopping. Doing these sorts of things helps children develop their muscles and their co-ordination. This is important for their physical development. Children enjoy physical activity with adults, throwing and kicking a ball, playing chase and play wrestling can be great fun! So try to find opportunities to do these things with your child.

Many of the games children play, especially as they get older, involve **rules.** Children have to learn how to follow the rules of games and like every other skill they need some help with this. The very simple games which young children play help them learn about rules. Games such as pass the parcel, have rules such as taking your turn and passing objects from one person to another and are a useful way to help children start to learn about rules in games. As children get older they will learn to play more complicated games such as board and card games. Taking time to play these sorts of games with your children is important as they need help to learn about the rules. These sorts of activities can also help your children learn important lessons for life in general. Think about the number of situations in everyday life where you have to wait your turn.

In **MAKE BELIEVE PLAY** children use pretend things rather than real things in their play.

Children create imaginary friends or fantasy situations like being on a desert island. Some adults feel that such fantasy play is silly and may even be bad for children but in fact it is just the opposite. Fantasy play gives children the opportunity to imagine what different situations are like and how they would feel and behave in those situations. It gives them the chance to think themselves into someone else's shoes and imagine what that feels like. In this way they can become sensitive to how other people might think and feel. It also helps children get a better idea of what is real and what is not. Give your child some dressing up clothes. Some of your old things or fun clothes you find at a jumble sale or grandma gives you. Play dressing up with your children and help them think of different people they can be in different situations.

Play is an important activity for learning and developing in every area of life.

Children need practice at playing in order to become good at it and creative in their play. This is where we come in as adults. By encouraging children to take part in all the different types of play described and by playing with our children as well we can help them get the most out of their play.

PLAYING WITH YOUR CHILD

We know that if we leave children to it, they will play spontaneously to a certain extent, but they need someone to teach them how to play if they are going to get the full benefit from it. Unless an adult helps a child to learn how to play, they miss out on all the exciting and important skills which play allows them to develop. We know that children get a great deal out of playing with adults and that adults help children to learn by using all the different kinds of play described beforehand. Adults can help them learn how to solve problems, develop their imagination and build on their self-esteem.

When children are playing it is very tempting to leave them to it and to go and get on with something we want to do, or simply sit quietly with the newspaper or a book for a little while. In this way the child is ignored when they are doing something positive. By taking the opportunity to join in with your child when they are playing, you can help them learn as well as having some fun with them and giving them some positive

attention. Playing with your children is a good thing but it is important to think about what you are doing and how you are doing it. If you haven't played for some time it is easy to get carried away with what you are doing and forget that you are really there to play with your child. Re-discovering how to make a paper plane or building with lego can be so absorbing that you neglect to play with your child. The following example illustrates this:

EXAMPLE

A father and his son Robert are playing with Lego.

Father: I'm going to build a car with those wheels.

Robert: I want to make a train and I need the wheels.

Father continues making his car and finishes it. Robert looks around for something else to do now that his father has taken the wheels.

Father: I'm going to make a house now. What are you making?

Robert starts to throw the Lego around the room.

Father: What's wrong?
Come on and play, this is fun.

WATCH NOW, SON ..... DON'T COME TOO NEAR!

This father is clearly having a good time but his son isn't. As we discussed earlier, children look for attention from people. If they can't get positive attention they will settle for negative attention. The above is a good example of this. When Robert does not get attention for his suggestion about the play, he starts to misbehave and gets attention straight away. Because the father responds to his misbehaviour he encourages it.

Now let us look at an example of a parent responding to a child in a way which encourages and promotes positive play.

EXAMPLE

A little boy is playing with his cars whilst his mother is reading a magazine.

Boy: Mummy, look at this (making the cars crash into each other).

Mother: (looks up from reading her magazine). Oh, the cars have crashed! Can I look at your cars (mum gets down on the floor with her son and looks at the cars) Oh look at this one, you can open the doors and the bonnet.

Boy: That's the engine inside isn't it. Do you know how it works?

Mother and son then look at the cars and talk about them and how they work.

Mother: You are looking at these really well. What else could we do with them?

Boy: We could have a race!

Mother: That's a good idea. Do you think we could make a race track around the room?

The little boy follows his mother's suggestions enthusiastically and makes a race circuit on the floor.

In this example the mother joins in with her son's game and helps him think of further things he can do with the cars. Notice how she praises him frequently whilst she is playing with him, by telling him that he is playing well with the cars and telling him that his ideas about playing with the cars are good. This will encourage him to think of further things to do with the toys. This mother has successfully played with her son and promoted his learning during this experience.

From these two examples you can see how the type of attention a child is given greatly affects behaviour. Providing positive attention for appropriate behaviour and ignoring inappropriate behaviour encourages children to behave in a positive way.

CONTROL AND COMPETITION

Sometimes adults compete with their children when they are playing, without knowing it.

They get into arguments about who won the game or what the rules are; they try to control the play all the time.

EXAMPLE

A father and son are drawing together.

Son: I'm going to draw a horse.

Father: I'll draw one for you and then you can copy it.

Son: But I know how to draw a horse.

Father: Well, if I draw it first then you are sure to get it right.

The little boy starts to doodle on his paper whilst his father draws a picture of a horse. When the horse is finished, the little boy scribbles over it.

In this example the father is clearly controlling the play and is determined that the child will do it his way. If this game carries on like this it is likely the child will get bored and will start to be disruptive. How else do you think the father could have managed this situation?

EXAMPLE

A mother and daughter are playing together in the living room.

Girl: I want to play with my Barbie doll and her clothes.

Mother: O.K. I'll get them out of the toy cupboard for you.

Girl: I want to get them out.

Mother: I don't think that is a good idea, you make such a mess. I'll get them out and then you can play with them.

Girl: (sulking) I don't want to play with them any more.

This mother is trying to control the play. Mother and daughter quickly become frustrated as they fight over who is going to to get the toys out of the cupboard. How else could this mother have managed this situation? One possibility is that she and her daughter could have gone to the toy cupboard together and mother could have helped her daughter to get the toys out. In this way she would have been helping her rather than discouraging her.

It is important to remember when you are playing with children that they have ideas about the games and want to control them. This will show them that you think their ideas are good and that they are fun to play with.

In the next examples you will see parents who are allowing their children to lead and to exercise their imaginations.

EXAMPLE

A father and son are playing with a racetrack and cars.

Son: I am going to put all my cars by the start line so they are ready for the race.

Father: That's a good idea. I'll line mine up behind yours.

Son: What can we do with the buildings (picks up the model garages).

Father: What do you think we could do with them?

Son: We could make them the place where the cars go to get their tyres changed.

Father: That's a great idea.

Father and son continue building their racetrack and then go on to have a race.

This father is following his son's lead and encouraging his imagination. This is a satisfying experience for both father and son. The father is helping his son to think about what he can do with the toys and the son is enjoying his father's attention.

EXAMPLE

A father and son are playing with some sticks they have collected whilst out walking. The father is encouraging the little boy to think about what he could do with the sticks.

Father: How many sticks did we get?

Son: (Counts the sticks). We got thirty.

Father: That's a lot of sticks. What shall we do with them?

Son: We could make wigwams out of the sticks.

Father: That's an interesting idea. Who lives in wigwams.

Son: Indians do and we could make a big wigwam for the grown up Indians and a small one for the children.

Father: That's a great idea.

Here the father follows his son's lead and praises him for his interesting idea. In this way he is encouraging his son's imagination. You can just see them going on to build the wigwams and playing a game with imaginary Indians!

In both these examples the parents have gone along with the children's ideas and encouraged them to develop them further. They have fostered the children's imaginations and have allowed them to take control of the play.

Playing with hyperactive children involves doing all the things described above but you will have to work hard to keep their attention on activities. When a child looses interest in their toy our natural reaction is to go and get something else or even to buy more toys. This does not solve the problem as the child seems to get bored just as quickly. The secret here is not to keep buying more toys but to play with your child and help them think of more things they can do with the toy. Suggest things they could do with the toy and encourage them to use their imagination.

SUMMARY

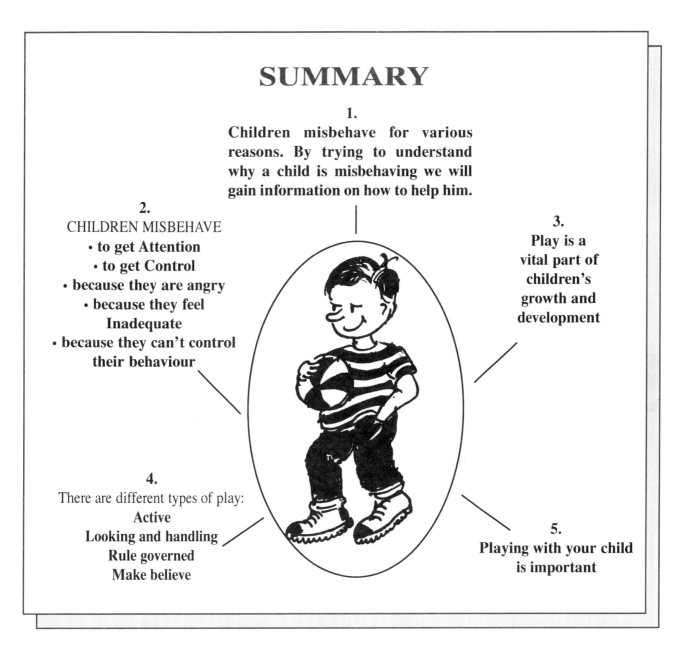

1.
Children misbehave for various reasons. By trying to understand why a child is misbehaving we will gain information on how to help him.

2.
CHILDREN MISBEHAVE
• to get Attention
• to get Control
• because they are angry
• because they feel
Inadequate
• because they can't control
their behaviour

3.
Play is a vital part of children's growth and development

4.
There are different types of play:
Active
Looking and handling
Rule governed
Make believe

5.
Playing with your child is important

TASK

Using the information about play that we have discussed in this chapter, try the following exercise.

Play with your child for a minimum of 10-15 minutes each day.
Keep track of these play periods on the Work Sheet: Play Times.

WORK SHEET: SPECIAL PLAY TIMES

DATE / TIME   **ACTIVITY**

27

5. COMMUNICATING WITH YOUR CHILD

Good communication is the basis of any good relationship. In order to build and maintain a positive relationship with someone we have to communicate well with them. Communication is quite complicated, it involves the words we use, the way we use them and our non-verbal communication (facial expression and body posture). In this chapter we are going to look at some basic communication skills and then discuss how to use these skills to communicate with children.

All parents talk to their children but, if you stop and listen to the way they do this it is likely that a lot of what they say will involve them nagging and criticising their children or even making fun of them. In the face of this, the child is unlikely to want to talk to their parent or if they do they may say something nasty or critical in response, as a way of getting their own back. Imagine what would happen if you talked to other adults in this way! They would not be very impressed and would think that you were quite rude. Think about how you like to be spoken to and then try speaking in that way to your child. Children tend to copy what they see and hear adults doing, so if you want your child to speak nicely to you and not swear at you or be cheeky to you, set him a good example, don't be cheeky to him.

BASIC COMMUNICATION SKILLS

There are three important components of basic communication which we will discuss in this section.

Words

Listening

Body Language

WORDS

First, let us think about the words we use when we talk. This is particularly important when you are talking to small children; you have to use words which they understand. Think about how you feel when someone uses a word which you do not fully understand and then think about this from your child's point of view. When we are talking to children the rule is to keep it simple, and if you think he might not have understood what you said, ask him - "do you know what that means" or "did you get what I was talking about there?" - use your own language, but check out with your child that

he is clear about what you have said.

Another very basic but important aspect of communication is that of not wasting words! We are probably all guilty of doing this. Talking at children, telling them to do things or nagging and criticising them can become second nature if you have a child with behaviour problems. The danger of doing this however, is that the child will start to ignore you. He will know that you say a lot and maybe even threaten things but you never do anything about it. Not surprising then that he ignores you. When we talk without expecting our children to listen to us, we are encouraging them to "turn a deaf ear" or become "parent deaf". Don't waste your words. Think about what you are going to say to your child and treat every word you use as a precious tool. If you do this, your child will take more notice of you when you do say something. Don't waste your words.

The next thing about words is to think about what you are saying and what effect it has on the person who hears it. Some of the things we say encourage people to keep talking and to tell us about things - these are called **open responses**. Other things will shut people up very quickly - these are called **closed responses**. The trick with communication is to know when to use an open response and when to use a closed response.

For Example:

Closed Responses:

Child: I hate school; there's no one to play with.

Mother: Oh don't be so silly.

This response ignores what the child is feeling. Communication with the child is not encouraged by this response and the child will be left feeling as though his mother does not understand and does not care enough to want to help him.

Open Responses:

Child: I hate school; there's no one to play with.

Mother: It sounds to me as though something has upset you at school. Would you like to tell me about it?

This response shows that the mother understands how her child is feeling and wants to help. This sort of response will also encourage the child to say more about how he feels.

LISTENING

Listening is a vital part of good communication. To be a good communicator you have to be a good listener. How often do you criticise your child because, "he doesn't listen to me"? How often do you really listen to what your child is saying? In order to listen effectively we have to concentrate very hard. You will need to look at your child, establish eye contact and show him that you are listening by the way you are standing or sitting; "body language" is very important.

Listening is not just about **listening** to the words, it also involves trying to understand the **feelings** behind the words. We do this automatically in most cases but sometimes it is important to pay more attention to this aspect of communication. **Reflective listening** is a well recognised technique you can use to show your child that you recognise what they are feeling. It will help your relationship with your child by showing him that you are listening to him, that you are tuned in to how he is feeling and that you can cope with his feelings. In addition, you will be helping him by actually saying what the feeling is. A very important part of helping our children to grow up is to help them understand and put names to the feelings they have.

When children get upset we can help them think through why they are upset by using reflective listening. To do this we reflect to the child what he is feeling and label it for him.

Here is an example.

Child: Paul always tells lies about me. It's not fair.

Mother: It sounds to me as though you are feeling angry and fed up with Paul.

Here the mother understands what her child is feeling and has put it into words for him.

REMEMBER that communication is always **verbal** and **non-verbal**. Our behaviour, our facial expressions and our tone of voice say a great deal. We can communicate a great deal by moving closer to a child, smiling or frowning.

Noticing your child's behaviour and non-verbal communication is another useful way of showing him that you are trying to understand him. Acknowledge non-verbal cues as well as verbal cues - for example.

"You look as though you are really upset. Do you want to tell me about it?"

You will probably feel a bit uncomfortable at first using the techniques we have discussed here. People often say that they "feel silly" using reflective listening. Reflecting back what the child has said to you is important, it is a way of helping him to understand what he is feeling. As far as feeling silly goes, it is always difficult when we start something new; it will feel strange and even uncomfortable for a while. However, with practice it will get easier, it will feel more familiar and eventually it will become second nature.

Your child will probably be surprised when you first use these communication techniques. It will take a little while for him to get used to it. If he doesn't respond the first time you try this, don't give up, try again next time you have the opportunity. Eventually you will both get used to it.

Most of the techniques described in this book will take a while before they bring results. It is important however, that you don't give up, keep trying. Your children are used to you behaving the way you have done in the past and it will take them a while to get used to the new ways.

PRACTICE AND PATIENCE are two of the essential ingredients for success.

Remember to watch what you are doing; it is possible to overdo reflective listening. So take some time to think about what is the right thing to say or whether you should just listen. You know your child well enough to know when he wants to talk and when you should leave him alone.

Sometimes children use problems to get attention. They keep coming back to you about the same thing. Obviously you want to help your child but you don't want to give him too much attention for this sort of behaviour. In these situations you could say something like:

"We have talked about this several times already. I think that you can handle it by yourself now."

BODY LANGUAGE

We have mentioned this briefly already. Communication is not just about the words we speak, it also involves body language, facial expression, body posture, eye contact etc. What you do with your body whilst you are listening and talking to someone can communicate a great deal.

EYE CONTACT

Looking at someone when you are talking to them instantly makes what you are saying more powerful. Think about how you feel when someone does not look at you when they talk to you, or when they won't look at you when you are talking to them. If you have something important to say and you want to be sure that someone is listening to you, make sure that you are looking at them and that they are looking at you.

You must be careful not to overdo eye contact, don't stare people out - be sensitive to the amount of eye contact you make.

It is very important to make eye contact with your child when you are speaking to him, especially if you are asking him to do something or telling him something you really want him to take notice of. If he does not look at you then don't say any more. Go over to him and try and make eye contact again. Actions speak louder than words and going over to a child, establishing physical closeness and looking at him is much more effective than yelling at him from the other side of the room. Body posture is also an important part of non -verbal communication. You can show that you are paying attention to someone by the way you are sitting or standing. Altering the position of your body so that you are facing the person is important. Trying to be as relaxed as possible is also good for facilitating communication. If someone thinks that you are relaxed then they are more likely to talk to you than if they think that you are anxious. Your children will be very sensitive to how you feel so they will soon know if you are paying attention properly or not really listening: if they think you aren't listening they are more likely to start to do something to get your attention - i.e. something you don't want them to do. Children also pick up if we are anxious about something. This usually has the effect of making them anxious which in turn often results in their behaviour deteriorating. Children get scared if they think their parents can't cope with a situation. This is why it is very important that you practice being calm. Even though you might not feel calm inside, try and show your child that you are in control.

Lets move on to look at some further aspects of comunication.

Good communication is very important in situations where there is a problem. An important first step in managing these situations is to work out what the problem is and who the problem belongs to. Getting this right helps you move on to the next step which is resolving the problem. The idea of thinking about problems in this way has been used by several experts in helping parents to manage childhood behavioural problems. The basic principles are described in the following section.

In order to determine who a problem belongs to, try thinking about the following questions:

1. **Who is experiencing the difficulty with whom?**

2. **Who is not getting what they want?**

For example:

a. **The child is not getting his own way. He is upset about this. It is not the adult's problem. The child owns the problem.**

b. **The child is getting his own way but his behaviour is a problem to the adults. The adult owns the problem.**

31

c. The child is getting what he wants and his behaviour does not interfere with the adults. Nobody has a problem.

Once you have worked out who owns the problem you can do something about it. If the problem belongs to the child you can talk it through with him and help him work out the best solution. If the problem belongs to you, then you must think carefully about how to proceed. Think about how you can solve the problem, there will often be more than one possible solution. So, think through the options and make a decision about what to do based on what is best for you and your child and for your relationship, remembering that what you do has an effect on your child.

Another technique, which is very effective, but which often we aren't good at doing is telling children how we feel. It is important to let children know when we are upset about something they are doing or if something they are doing is making us angry. It is also very important that we tell them when we are happy about something or we like something that they have done. In this way we can help children think about the effect of their behaviour on other people without being critical or blaming them and making them feel bad about themselves.

For example:

"When you jump up and down on the sofa I get concerned because you might fall and hurt yourself".

and

I really like it when you help your brother like that. It makes me happy to see you do that.

The technique here is all about talking about yourself and saying how you feel rather than talking about your child. In this way you don't blame or criticise him, instead you help him understand the effect he has on other people when he does things. You are in fact helping him to consider other people's feelings. Hyperactive children have great difficulties with this. They are impulsive and so they tend to rush in without thinking about the effect of what they are doing on other people. So using this technique will help them tremendously in learning to think first before they act.

Using this technique is quite simple and involves you:-

Describing the behaviour which is interfering with you - it is important that you just describe it and that you don't criticise.

e.g. "You guys are playing very loudly"

Stating how you feel:

"I am angry because I can't hear what is being said on the phone".

This is much more effective than criticising your child and telling him off because he is doing something wrong.

e.g. **"You are very naughty when you make so much noise".**

It is o.k. to get angry with your child but as with everything else, the way you do it is important.

Before you start getting angry with your child, it is important that you think first about why you are angry. It is usually not the child's behaviour itself which is annoying you but rather the consequences of his behaviour, because it in some way interferes with you and what you are doing. If the child's behaviour did not have these consequences, you probably would not be bothered by it.

For example:

You are making dinner and your children are in the other room playing and making a lot of noise. Their noise does not bother you. The phone rings. You answer and you cannot hear what is being said because of the noise. Now their behaviour does annoy you; it is interfering with your needs.

So, remember to think about whether it is your child's behaviour or the consequences of the behaviour (the effect of the behaviour on you) that is making you angry. When you tell your child how you feel about his behaviour, remember to tell him it is the consequences of his behaviour which is upsetting you not the child himself.

SUMMARY

◆ Communication involves listening to your child and showing him that you understand.

◆ In order to listen effectively we need to establish eye contact and adopt a posture which shows that we are listening.

◆ Try not to nag, lecture, criticise or make fun of your child.

◆ Talk to your child in the way you would like him to talk to you.

◆ Remember to respect your child.

◆ Reflective listening involves hearing what your child has said and the feelings behind it and saying it back to him so he feels understood.

◆ Try to use open responses not closed responses.

◆ Help your child to think about the consequences of his actions by telling him how it makes you feel.

TASK

Practice using reflective listening, problem ownership and telling your child how his behaviour makes you feel. Make a note of the situations in which you use these techniques and what the effect on your child is on the Work Sheet: Communication Techniques.

WORK SHEET: COMMUNICATION TECHNIQUES

TECHNIQUE	SITUATION	CHILD'S RESPONSE

6. ENCOURAGING POSITIVE BEHAVIOUR

In order to encourage positive behaviour we have to praise and reward children when they do something that we like and that is positive. This will make it more likely that the child will behave in the same way again in the future. People often think that "reward" means something material, money or a present of some sort. It does not have to be. Adult attention and praise are very powerful rewards. We can use praise and rewards to encourage and strengthen positive behaviour.

It is easy to use praise; hugs, smiles and other forms of non-material reward are important. We all like to be praised and to feel that someone values us. It is however, very easy to forget to praise children (and adults) when they do simple things which we take for granted such as playing quietly or saying "thank you". The danger is that we only praise children when they have done something really good.

Children thrive on praise. Children who are not praised or given attention for positive behaviours are more likely to misbehave. So praise is very important in encouraging positive behaviour. Children need to be praised if they are to think positively about themselves and to develop a positive self-concept (we will talk more about this in Chapter 7). We can also use praise to encourage children to learn new skills and to help their self esteem. Praise is cheap, it doesn't cost a thing and it can have a dramatic effect on a child's behaviour.

There follows a description of the different aspects of giving praise illustrated with examples.

HOW AND WHEN TO USE PRAISE

It is important to praise children for everyday things as well as when they do something really well. Remember that a child will be much more likely to repeat a behaviour if he has been praised for it than if it has been ignored. Think of all the things you would like to see your child do more often and praise him when he does them. On many occasions such things go unrewarded. Parents often think that children should not need praise and that they should know how to behave without being praised. This is not the case.

EXAMPLE

A mother is helping her two sons, Thomas, aged 5 and Jamie, aged 3 years to get ready for bed. They are getting undressed ready for their bath. Thomas goes to the washing basket and puts his clothes in.

Mother: Thomas, that was so good, you put your dirty clothes in the washing basket. That was really helpful, thank you.

Thomas: (Smiles at his mother, pleased to have been praised). I am going to do that every day.

Mother: That's a really good idea, and it will help me so much if you do that.

Jamie: I will do that too Mummy.

Mother: Thank you Jamie. I am so lucky to have two helpful boys like you. (Mother gives both boys a hug and a kiss).

Here the mother is doing a very good job giving praise and attention to both of her children. She labels what they have done to please. She also makes good use of physical contact, a hug and a kiss to emphasise how pleased she is with the boys. The children are obviously pleased to have made their mother so happy and are enjoying the praise she has given them.

EXPLAINING PRAISE

In the above example the mother used praise in an effective way. She was enthusiastic and praised the activities of her children. She also told her children why she was pleased with them. Sometimes parents use praise in a non-specific way. They say things like "good boy" and "well done". Why is he a good boy and what has he done well? Telling a child why you are praising him will help him learn about the behaviour you like.

In the next examples parents explain why they are praising their children.

EXAMPLE

It is dinner time and a mother is trying to get her two boys Michael aged five and Tony aged three to sit at the table for their meal.

Mother: O.K. boys, it's time for dinner. Come and sit at the table please.

(Michael and Tony continue their game of running around the sitting room after each other).

Mother: Boys, come and sit down now or you will not get any dinner.

Michael: O.K. mum. (Michael goes over to the table and sits down. Tony carries on running around giggling.)

Mother: Well done Michael, you are sitting very well.

Mother ignores Tony and continues to chat to Michael praising him for his behaviour. Tony realises that his brother is getting attention and goes to sit down at the table.

Mother: Oh Tony, well done you have come to join us, that is nice, now we can all have our meal together.

This mother does well in praising Michael as soon as he does as she asks and explaining why she is pleased with him. She ignores Tony who does not do as she asks at first. When Tony sees that his brother is getting all the attention he comes over to the table. His mother immediately praises him and again explains why she is pleased. In this way, Mother gets both children to come to the table without shouting at either of them. She remains calm throughout.

PRAISING EFFORT

Sometimes we expect too much of our children and fail to reward their efforts. This will discourage them and they will give up trying. If we wait too long or only reward a child when he does something perfectly, we will undermine his self-confidence and put him off trying. Sometimes parents become so concerned that their child does something perfectly that they end up punishing him for his efforts rather than encouraging him to try.

EXAMPLE

Victoria who is 5 years old is trying to put her toys away in their boxes and then into the toy cupboard when mum comes in.

Mother: Victoria, if you are going to put your toys away, at least try not to make such as mess. Look at the state of the cupboard.

Victoria: I was just trying to tidy up and help.

Mother: It is such a mess. Nobody will be able to find anything. The cupboard looks like a disaster area.

This mother is very upset because of the way her daughter is trying to put away the toys. The toy cupboard looks untidy. She has failed to acknowledge that her child is trying to tidy up and to be helpful. She criticises her and in effect punishes her for her efforts. This mum missed the opportunity to reward a useful behaviour and to develop a skill.

In this respect it is important to reward attempts at constructive, useful, positive behaviour even though they may not be very skilled. It is then possible to build on the attempts and use the experience to develop new skills.

It is easy to make mistakes when trying to praise children. One of the commonest mistakes is to give praise with one hand and take it away with the other by criticising. Praise is only effective in reinforcing a behaviour, (that is making it more likely that it will happen again) if the praise is given immediately after the behaviour.

The following examples illustrate some of the traps:

EXAMPLE

A father and his two sons, John and David, are getting ready to go out for a walk.

Father: Come on boys, get your shoes and coats on; then we can go.

John: O.K. Dad (John starts to put his shoes on).

Father: Hurry up John, you take so long with your shoes. David what are you doing?

David: I'm coming. Where is my coat?

Father: For goodness sake David, your coat is where we always put it, hanging up.

John: I'm ready.

Father: At last. David, we'll go without you.

David: I'm ready.

This father is being highly critical of both his children. He missed several opportunities to reward their compliance and to praise their efforts. By behaving in this way, he is not encouraging his children to comply with his requests, nor is he encouraging good behaviour.

EXAMPLE

A mother and her two children Derrick and Donna have been to their grandmother's house for lunch. Both children behaved very well and ate all the food their grandmother gave them.

Mother: I am very pleased with both of you. You behaved very well. I was really pleased that you ate all your lunch. Granny thought that was great.

Donna: I enjoyed it at Granny's today.

Derrick: So did I.

Mother: Yes well, its just a pity that the two of you don't behave like that all the time - particularly at home.

Both children look down cast and don't say anything more to their mother on the way home.

This mother starts off doing well in praising her children and telling them that she is pleased with their behaviour at Granny's. The children are obviously pleased with this and looking forward to going to Granny's again. Mum unfortunately goes on to spoil things by criticising the children's behaviour at other times. By doing this she has undone all the good she did in praising her children. It is important that, when you have given praise to a child for something, you do not then take the praise away by being critical about something else.

HOW DO CHILDREN DEAL WITH PRAISE?

Sometimes parents worry that giving their children praise is bad for them, that they will become big headed and spoiled and need praise all the time. This is not the case. Children who are praised appropriately, grow in self-confidence and self-esteem and need less praise because they are more sure of themselves.

CHILDREN WHO CAN'T HEAR PRAISE

Some children seem to find it very hard to hear praise. They respond to praise by misbehaving or doing something which makes you feel as though they are punishing you for praising them. These children tend to have low self-esteem and so find it hard to hear anyone saying nice things about them. It is as though they don't believe people who think they are good at something. They seem to be testing you to see if you really mean the nice things you said about them.

In this situation it is best to avoid arguing with the child about the praise. Just give the praise and ignore any inappropriate response from the child. It is very important to continue to give praise to these children. Don't give up because they reject your praise. It will take some time before a child with low self-esteem feels good enough about himself to accept your praise.

PHYSICAL CONTACT

Remember that adding a cuddle or a kiss when you praise your child will make it much more effective. A hug together with lots of verbal praise is much nicer than just the praise.

USING REWARDS

The use of rewards is another important technique for encouraging positive behaviour. Rewards are something concrete, such as putting stars on a chart, doing something special with parents or special treats such as toys or money. They can be used to help children to learn difficult things such as new skills or to control problem behaviours. It is not a good idea to rely on rewards alone; it is much more effective if both praise and rewards are used.

Rewards can be given:

As a surprise - when the child has done really well he should be rewarded for doing so. As we discussed before, it is important to label the behaviour the child is being rewarded for.

or **Planned in advance** - here the child is told exactly what behaviour will result in a reward. This is like making a deal with a child.

SURPRISE REWARDS

When a child has done something very well, it is good to show him that you recognise how hard he has worked. You can do this by giving him a special treat which he was not expecting.

EXAMPLE

John, who is four and a half, has been helping his mother put away the ironing.

Mother: Thank you for helping me tidy up the ironing. I really appreciate it. Since you helped me so well with that job, as a special treat, would you like a choc bar?

John: (very excited) Yes please!

Note that this mother uses praise and an unexpected material reward. She is very enthusiastic with her verbal praise which adds emphasis. Notice that she labels the activity she is praising.

PLANNED REWARDS

You can use rewards to encourage a child to do something you want them to do. You can promise them a special reward if they do what you ask. It is important not to confuse planned rewards with bribes. The main difference between a bribe and a reward is:

a bribe is given to try to make someone do something whereas a reward is given to someone when they have done something.

EXAMPLE

Two young boys are playing noisily on the floor with toy cars. Their mother is about to make a telephone call.

Mother: Boys, you can have a biscuit if you play nicely while I am on the telephone. The packet is on the table. Help yourselves. Just one each.

The boys proceed to take a biscuit and jump around making a lot of noise whilst the mother is on the phone.

This mother tried unsuccessfully to bribe her children to be quiet whilst she made a telephone call. She gave the reward before the desired behaviour occurred. In the end what she rewarded was the undesirable behaviour; the children got a biscuit and enjoyed themselves jumping around.

What she could have done was:

Mother: If you can play nicely and quietly whilst I am making this telephone call, then, when I have finished I will give you both a biscuit.

Here the mother makes it clear what she wants the children to do and what the reward will be if they achieve that behaviour. It is an example of the **First / Then Rule.**

THE FIRST / THEN RULE

In the above you saw an example of the **First / Then Rule.**

Basically this states that **FIRST** you get the appropriate behaviour. **THEN** the child gets the reward - as follows:

EXAMPLE

A father is working in the kitchen when his son comes through from the living room where he has been playing with his computer game.

Son: Will you come outside and play football with me Dad?

Father: Yes, I'd like that but **FIRST** tidy up your computer game **THEN** we'll go outside O.K.

The little boy proceeds to tidy up in the living room and he and his father then go outside to play.

Here the father very clearly uses the **First / Then Rule.** His son readily complies with his father's request.

STAR CHARTS

Star charts can be used to help children with their behaviour. Star charts are another form of material reward. Here the child is awarded a star (or a smiley face) when he shows the desired behaviour. In order for star charts to work the child has to be involved from the beginning. It is essential to explain to the child that if he manages to do whatever it is you want, he will get a star. The chart should be put up in a convenient place; people often find that the kitchen is a good place. When the desired behaviour occurs, it is important to praise the child for doing well and tell him that, because he performed the desired behaviour, you are going to give him a star to put on his chart. You decide whether or not he gets the star, but it is nice to allow the child to put the star on the chart.

In order for this technique to work, the child must be able to achieve something. If your child is not managing to get any stars he will quickly get fed up and feel as though he is never going to be able to do what you want. It is very likely that he will give up and stop trying. If your child has not got any stars, try adjusting what you expect of him so that he can get some stars.

Star chart programmes can be developed to add in further material rewards, for example, if the child gets more than a certain number of stars in one week (again, this number is decided by you) then he has a further reward, which is a special treat which you decide. The treat should be something which is very special to the child. It can involve money - for example a toy, sweets, a trip to the cinema or McDonald's, or, better still it can involve doing something with you which he particularly enjoys - such as a game of football or helping you to wash the car.

EXAMPLE

A mother and her daughter, Susan, are sitting in their living room.

Mother: I have noticed that you have been finding it hard to go to bed lately. You remember last night when you came down stairs all those times and daddy and I got cross with you? I think it would be better if we could help you go to bed and not get up again. So, what I thought we could do is make a chart for you. If you manage to go to bed and don't come down stairs again, daddy and I will give you a star to go on your chart. When you have 5 stars on your chart, then you can get to make scones with me.

Susan: Can we make some now?

Mother: No, remember I said that you need 5 stars before we make scones.

Susan: O.K.

Mother: I am really looking forward to making scones with you. (smiling at her daughter)

This mother is setting up a star chart to help her child with bed time. She takes time to explain what is going to happen and makes sure that the child has understood. The child is happy with the idea of the chart and is looking forward to baking with her mother.

Once your child is achieving what you want and is getting lots of stars, the time has come to make it harder for him to get stars or to move on to a different behaviour.

EXAMPLE

Toby and his family have been using a Star Chart to help Toby with his problems sharing with his younger brother David.

Father: Toby you have been sharing really well with David for the last two weeks, I notice that your Star Chart has been full and you got your special treat twice now. I think that maybe this is too easy for you now, so we should make things a little tougher for you. Instead of you needing five stars for a special treat I think we should make it ten. What do you think?

Toby: That's easy, I bet I still get my special treat.

Father: That's great Toby, it sounds as though you feel really confident. I am sure that you can do it as well.

Father has carefully explained to his son about making it harder for him to get his special treat. He has explained this in a way which compliments and praises his son for how well he has done so far. This little boy seems to be really enthusiastic about the whole process and seems determined to continue to do well. He has obviously enjoyed the praise and rewards he has achieved so far.

REMEMBER

Use praise, hugs and kisses.

Don't wait for the child to get it right all the way before giving a reward.

 Use praise for small steps in the right direction.

Keep the rewards interesting. Change the rewards now and then.

 Clearly define the behaviour you want to see more of.

Make sure your child achieves something.

As your child gets better at the behaviour, increase what he has to do to get the reward.

Don't try to change too much at once.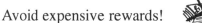

 Concentrate on positive behaviours.

Avoid expensive rewards!

Let your child help you to make the chart.

TASK

1. Practice using praise. A good time to do this is during your 15 minutes **Special Play** time with your child.

2. Record the situations in which you praise your child and note how he responds on Work Sheet 1: Praises.

3. Make a list of those behaviours you would like to see more of on Work Sheet 2. Hoped For Behaviours.

4. Choose one behaviour and systematically praise it every time it occurs over the next week.

5. Choose one behaviour and set up a star chart Work Sheet 3 to encourage the behaviour to happen more.

WORK SHEET 1: PRAISES

SITUATION **CHILD'S RESPONSE TO PRAISE**
(Why praise was given
 and how it was given)

WORK SHEET 2: HOPED FOR BEHAVIOURS

On this sheet make a list of all those behaviours your child shows which you would like to see more of. Choose one of these behaviours and reward it every time it occurs.

45

WORK SHEET 3: STAR CHART

On this sheet record the details of the Star Chart you are going to set up with your child.

Target Behaviour

Star Chart ★	Before breakfast	Before lunch	Before dinner	Before supper
Monday ★				
Tuesday ★				
Wednesday ★				
Thursday ★				
Friday ★				
Saturday ★				
Sunday ★				

This is an example of a simple Star Chart showing days of the weeks and days divided up into periods of time. Obviously the sort of chart you will need will depend on the behaviour you are targeting.

Encourage your child to work towards getting a star by improving his behaviour.

7. SELF-CONFIDENCE, YOUR OWN AND YOUR CHILD'S

SELF-CONCEPT

Self-concept, that is what a person thinks about themselves, is important in determining the way they behave. That is to say, how we feel about ourselves will affect the way we behave.

Self-concept consists of all the things we think about ourselves, who we are, what we do, what we stand for, what we don't do. All those things which make us individuals, different from everybody else. People who have a good self-concept believe that they are worthwhile, that they are able to do things and to do them reasonably well. They feel that they are just as important as other people. A person who has a poor self-concept, feels as though they can't do anything right, that they are not good enough and that they are not important.

Self-concept is something which we develop through our interactions with other people throughout our lives. It begins when we are small. We learn from the approval or disapproval of other people (particularly those people who are important to us such as our parents and family) whether we are valuable as a human being.

This section of the book is all about self-confidence, self-esteem and self-concept. What you think about yourself as a person and also what your child thinks about himself.

It would be my guess that both you and your child, quite often, don't think very much of yourselves. That is, you both have poor self-esteem and poor self-confidence. You don't rate yourselves very highly. Some days are better than others. Some days, when things mostly seem to go well, you feel better about yourself, and the same goes for your child. When he has a good day he feels OK about himself.

We are going to look at ways in which both you and your child can build your self-esteem and self-confidence so that you have a good self-concept. Remember that the way you feel affects the way you behave. The way you behave affects your child. So if you feel good about yourself you will radiate this to your child who in turn will feel good about himself.

The work of this chapter is divided into two sections, one about building your self-confidence, and the other about doing the same for your child. In general however, the work of both sections can be applied to you and your child.

BUILDING YOUR CONFIDENCE

Let us start by considering the things that affect the way you feel about yourself. We can then look at what we can do to help you think more positively about yourself.

It is important that you try to think positively about yourself in spite of what goes on round about you. You must respect yourself and recognise that you are an effective person. Sometimes it is hard to think this way. In fact many people find it difficult to think about themselves at all, other than to find fault with themselves. Let's start by finding out what you think about yourself. Try and make a list of all your strengths, that is all the things that you like about yourself or that you think you do well. What are the things you value about yourself? Your patience, sense of humour, kindness?

LIST
My strengths
1. ....
2. ....
3. ....
4. ....
5. ....
6. ....
7. ....
8. ....
9. ....

It is likely that you found this quite hard. Sometimes when we do this exercise with people, they can't think of anything positive to say about themselves. If I had asked you to make a list of all your negative qualities, (your bad points) you would probably have been able to fill a page. If you are struggling to think of any good qualities, ask your partner or a friend what they think about you.

Hold on to your list, as time goes on, and you become more confident and positive about yourself, you will be able to add more things.

We often allow what happens to us day-to-day, to affect how we feel about ourselves. Something goes wrong and we feel as though we are a failure. On the other hand when something goes well we feel pleased with ourselves and more confident. Often what happens day-to-day has little to do with who you are and so it should not be used as a measuring stick against which to judge yourself as a person.

If you base your feelings of self-worth on what goes on from day to day then you are in danger of feeling quite badly about yourself. Some of the things which happen day-to-day are completely outwith your control and have nothing to do with your abilities or who you are as a person. Things just happen! For example, during the time that you are working through this book you will find that progress is a bit up and down. One week things will seem to be going well, the next, you feel as though you have gone backwards. Remember that progress is up and down. Even when you have finished the book you will find that the road is not completely smooth. You will go through some bumpy patches. It is important during these times to remember that even though you feel as though you have gone backwards, you are in fact still further ahead than you were when you started and you are learning from all these set-backs.

It is also important to be realistic about what you expect of yourself and other people. Sometimes people set goals for themselves or standards they expect of themselves which are impossible to achieve. They then feel bad about themselves when they don't achieve the goal or meet the standard. If a person repeatedly fails to achieve they are at risk of feeling bad about themselves and their self-esteem will suffer.

FEELING BADLY ABOUT YOURSELF

Thinking badly about yourself will undermine your self-confidence. If you consider yourself to be a failure you are in danger of setting yourself up to fail. If you think that you are not good enough and that you can't do something then you are less likely to succeed. If you think positively about yourself and that you are capable of doing something you are more likely to succeed. So, it is important to think positively about yourself and think that you can do things.

OTHER PEOPLE AND HOW TO DEAL WITH THEM

It is very likely that you will hear criticism from other people about the behaviour of your child and what you are doing. It is also likely that when this happens it will make you feel badly about yourself. You might feel demoralised by this criticism. You may be tempted to tell them to mind their own business or, you may feel as though you want to give up what you are trying to do. You may want to shout angrily at them, or you may feel too fed up and tired to bother trying to explain the difficulties your child has and what you are trying to do.

When other adults criticise what you are

doing, think about it in this way. They are criticising you because they think they know better and could do it better than you. It is important that you remember that you are the expert as far as your child is concerned and the people who are criticising you do not know anything about what you are trying to do to help him.

When someone criticises you, there are a number of things you can do. You may choose to ignore them or you may feel that you want to say something to the person. Tell the person about the situation you are in, that you are trying to help your child with his behaviour. You could even tell the person how their criticism makes you feel. Stay calm, be polite, but at the same time point out to them that you know what you are doing and intend to carry on.

GUILT

The way your children behave can affect the way you feel about yourself. You may feel guilty if your child gets in a mess. It is important that you don't simply settle for feeling badly for your child. You must act on your feelings and try to do something to change things to help your child so that things don't go wrong again. Parents of hyperactive children are particularly at risk of feeling guilty about their children and feeling as though they have failed. Parents often ask if their child's difficulties are due to something that they have done. They are not, and it is important that as parents of hyperactive children, you maintain a positive attitude and see each set-back as the opportunity to learn something else about how you can help your child with their behavioural difficulties.

It is important that you spend some time and energy thinking about yourself and building your own sense of self-worth and self-respect. In this way you will build a strong sense of self-concept. If you feel positive and confident about yourself this will help you in everything you do, including helping your children.

BUILDING YOUR CHILD'S CONFIDENCE

Very often **children who suffer from hyperactivity have very low self-esteem.** They know that they get things wrong a lot of the time and are aware that other people, especially their families get tired and fed up of their behaviour. They don't feel very good about themselves. As we discussed earlier in the book, one reason why children misbehave is that they have poor self-esteem. They don't believe that they can get anything right and get attention for good behaviour and so they misbehave in order to get some attention.

We need to help children build their sense of self-worth and their self-concept. We must help them so that they develop their self-esteem and self-confidence. The changes we have discussed already will help with this. In particular it is important to remember to concentrate on the things about your child's behaviour that you like and to ignore or give very little attention to his mistakes. Try to adopt a **positive** approach to your child and praise even the smallest thing he does well.

It is important to remember that we can influence the behaviour of other people, through **our own behaviour.** Remember that relationships are two way things and that your behaviour affects the way other people behave. By changing your behaviour, you can influence the behaviour of your children.

So it is important to change some things about the way you behave in order for there to be change in the way your child behaves. This applies to the way you think about yourself and your self-esteem and self-confidence. If you believe in yourself and like yourself, it will show in the way you behave with your child. You will help him to believe in himself and like himself more.

Parents want the best for their children. Very often what happens day-to-day does not match what we would really like to see happen. It is easy to get stuck in a position of expecting the worst to happen and being discouraging towards ourselves and our children. We don't have to get stuck like this however.

Lets spend some time thinking about how you can help your child with their self esteem.

POSITIVE AND NEGATIVE EXPECTATIONS

Our expectations of children can have a very strong influence on the way they behave. If you believe that your children are going to do things badly and get in trouble, they will probably **"live down"** to your expectations. On the other hand, if you expect that they will try to do the best they can and accept their efforts, it is more likely that your children will try to do well.

Encourage your children in their efforts. This will improve their self esteem and help build on your relationship with your child - making it more positive. It will also help your own feelings of worth. If you don't have to spend so much time criticising and pointing out what your child has done wrong, you will have more time for the fun part of being a parent, enjoying your child and showing him that you love and value him.

HELPING CHILDREN TO SUCCEED

Hyperactive children so often get into difficulties because of their behaviour that very often their parents come to expect nothing else. You can help your child with this by taking some time to think about situations in which your child does well and succeeds and by trying to ensure that they succeed at something everyday. It is very important that you try to think positively and encourage your children. Think carefully about situations you are going to take them into, think about what the difficulties might be and try to find a way round them. Also try to put your children into situations where they can succeed and do well.

BE REALISTIC

Carrying on from what was said above, don't expect too much of your children. Don't expect them to be able to do things which grown-ups do. Think about the world from their point of view. This is very important for hyperactive children. You have to think about the world with their difficulties in mind and plan ways to help them succeed.

ALLOW CHILDREN TO TRY

Although it is important to try to help your children to succeed, it is important that you allow them to fail every now and then. This will help them to learn their own limitations and learn from their mistakes. There is a danger as a parent of a hyperactive child, that you might try to do everything for your child so as to stop him getting in a mess, or you may allow him to do only those things which you know he will get right. This will give him a very false idea of the world and his own abilities. So whilst you should encourage your children to do well, don't prevent them from experiencing failure as well.

RESPECT AND VALUE YOUR CHILDREN AS THEY ARE

Respect is very important in any relationship and it is important that we show children that we respect them for who they are, warts and all. Although you can probably see lots of ways in which you would like your child to be different or "improve" it is important that you show your children that you love and respect them for who they are now, not who they could be. If by your actions you let your child see that you don't like who they are, this will have a very negative effect on their self- esteem. They will dislike themselves even more and it is likely that their behaviour will get worse as a result.

Hyperactive children, because of their difficulties often do things which parents don't like. It is very important to separate their behaviour from them as people, and let your child know that it is his behaviour at times that you don't like and not him. You love and respect him, but sometimes you really don't like his behaviour. This is an important distinction, separating your child from his behaviour. Separating your child from his behaviour allows you to go on loving and respecting him but also being able to recognise

hose aspects of his behaviour which need some work.

PRAISE

In the last chapter we discussed the use of praise to promote positive behaviour. Praise is also very important when we are trying to build a child's self esteem. Praise your child whenever you can, tell him how well he is playing with his cars and how good he is for putting his dishes in the sink or putting his bag in the cupboard. Use the techniques we have discussed in earlier chapters which show your child that you respect him. Avoid interfering with your child when he is trying to work something out. This will undermine him and suggests that you do not think that he is good enough to solve a problem. Help him by encouraging him to think about how to solve things himself. This will show him that you think he is good enough. If you show your children that you believe in them they will come to believe in themselves. Let your child know that you are confident in him and point out his positive aspects and achievements and not his faults and mistakes.

It is important that children feel useful if they are to feel worthwhile. You can help your child to feel useful by helping him to find things that he is good at and encouraging him to use these skills.

ENCOURAGEMENT

It is important to encourage children for their efforts and praise them when they have tried to do something, not just when they succeed. When we only praise the final result children will feel that they are only good enough when they achieve perfection. When you see your child trying to do something help him in his efforts by encouraging him. Tell him that you think he has done well and that you are proud of him for trying. Look for other ways to encourage your child - don't miss any opportunity to comment on his efforts when you see him trying.

BE CAREFUL

Don't give with one hand and take away with the other. It is very easy to give a child encouragement and then undo all your good work by adding a comment at the end which undermines the child's efforts - such as:

You did really well today -

> *Why can't you be like that all the time?*

> *Pity you don't behave like that at home?*

BROTHERS AND SISTERS

If you have more than one child, it is important to think about the relationships between brothers and sisters. It is very easy to play one child off against the other without realising what you are doing. For example you may praise one child who has done really well and criticise the other because you think that they can do better. Whilst a little competition can be healthy, it can also be very destructive, especially if you have a child who has real difficulties with their behaviour and performance, such as a hyperactive child. Respect your children as individuals and acknowledge that one is good at one thing and the other is good at another thing but that you love and respect them both equally. In the case of hyperactive children this is particularly important. If they have a brother or sister who is a high achiever, they may become even more demoralised by their own difficulties. Help them to find things that they do really well and may even be better at than their brother or sister.

A word of warning

When we are working to change a "problem child's" behaviour it has an effect on the other children in the family. They are used to their brother/sister always getting into trouble and themselves being "the apple of their parents eye". As the "problem child" becomes less of a problem their brothers and sisters are faced with their position as "good children" being threatened. The chances are that they will, for a time try out a new role of being a "problem child". **DO NOT DESPAIR.** The switch to problem behaviour is usually temporary. As you continue to work in encouraging ways with all your children, the competition will decrease, your children will become more co-operative and will be less prone to trying to establish a place at the expense of each other.

SUMMARY

- Do whatever you can to become more self-confident.

- You do not get your feelings of worth from your children's behaviour.

- You are more interested in improving your relationship with your children than you are in achieving perfection.

- Value and accept children as they are.

- Point out their positive behaviour.

- Show your child that you have faith in him.

- Recognise effort and improvement - not just achievement.

- Show appreciation for contributions.

- Use encouragement as well as praise.

TASK

1. Continue with everything you are doing already.
2. Find ways to encourage your child. Notice what happens when you do.
   Make a note of this over the next week.

WORK SHEET: ENCOURAGING YOUR CHILD

On this sheet, record situations in which you were able to praise your child and record his response to your praise.

SITUATION

RESPONSE TO ENCOURAGEMENT

8. HELPING YOUR CHILD TO LEARN SELF CONTROL

This chapter marks the beginning of the section of the book which is specifically about behaviour management - the bit you have been looking forward to!

Before we start however, I want to remind you of the importance of the work we have already done. We have covered a great deal of ground so far, all of which is important in terms of developing your relationship with your child so that you are in the best position to help him with his behaviour problems. It will be very important that you carry on with all the new skills we have worked on so far; don't forget about them or let them slip. They are the ground work on which to build the remaining skills and behaviour management techniques which we are going to cover in the next few chapters.

In this chapter we will discuss how to **set limits** for children and how to help them think through the **consequences** of their behaviour. In this way we encourage positive behaviour and help children learn to control their own behaviour.

SETTING LIMITS

Children need our help to learn what is appropriate behaviour and what is not. As adults, we often make the mistake of expecting children to know the right way to behave. We then get angry and disappointed when they get it wrong and behave in a way which we don't like. Remember that your children have to learn about behaviour and they rely on adults, their parents in particular, to help them with this huge task.

One of the things we do to help children to learn about how to behave is to set limits for them. This is particularly important for very young children. As children get older we have to help them to learn to limit their own behaviour. Later in this chapter we are going to discuss how you can help children to limit their own behaviour by allowing them to make choices and experience the consequences of those choices. To begin with however, it will help your children if you set down some guidelines, some house rules if you like, about behaviour which is OK. and behaviour which is not.

When we are setting limits for children we have to try to get the balance right between too many rules and too few. If there are not enough rules, children get into trouble because they don't know what they are supposed to do and not to do. If there are too many rules, children may become overwhelmed and either rebel or become withdrawn. What you have to do is to set enough rules so that your children feel contained and can make decisions about what they are going to do knowing the ground rules.

There are no hard and fast rules about setting rules! You as the grown-ups have to make the decisions about the rules in your house - what is acceptable and what is not. It is very important that parents agree with each other about rules - remember how important consistency is. If one parent says no to something, the other must back this up, even if you don't necessarily agree. Children get confused if parents disagree about rules and when children are confused they get scared and their behaviour gets worse. So, work out between you what you expect in terms of behaviour from your child and what is and is not acceptable and then stick to it.

Setting rules is the first step in helping children learn how to control their behaviour. When children are very young we set limits for behaviour and stop children when they try to break the limit or the rule. As children get older we have to help them learn to control their own behaviour. One way to do this would be to punish them when their behaviour is not acceptable and reward them when we like what they do. Another way would be to help them think about the choices they have about how they behave, then help them to think through what will happen depending on how they choose to behave. Having thought about the various possibilities they can then make a choice about what they want to do. They must then live with the consequence of that choice. By using this technique we help children learn about the consequences of their actions. This is an important technique for children who are hyperactive. They tend to be very impulsive and so they need a lot of help to learn to think about the potential consequences of their actions.

CHOICES

Very often in life we have a choice of different courses of action. As adults we think through the various options (usually, but not always) and make a choice about what to do based on the consequences of our actions. It is just the same for children. They are also faced with choices. However, they are not as skilled as adults in taking time to think things through, especially, if they suffer from hyperactivity. They need help to consider the various courses of action, and this is where you as parents come in. Sensitive adults can help children think of alternatives and choose a solution which will have a positive result.

MAKING CHOICES or GIVING ADVICE

Helping a child look at choices should not be confused with giving advice. The two things are very different. Giving advice means that you are telling the child how you think he should solve the problem. Looking at choices on the other hand means that you are helping the child identify the options, consider them and then make a choice. You are helping him to think things through and not just presenting him with the solution. Remember that hyperactive children have difficulties thinking things through and so practicing looking at choices with your child will help him with this problem.

HELPING YOUR CHILD TO MAKE CHOICES

When your child is confronted with a situation in which he has to make a choice, you can help him with this by talking him through the process. Firstly you have to talk to your

child about what it is they have to make a choice about. Use the communication skills you learned about earlier in the book, such as reflective listening, to help with this. Once your child has told you what the situation is you can help him think what he could do to either solve the problem or resolve the situation. You should encourage your child to think of as many different options as possible. You must then help him to think of the consequences of all the options he has told you and then on the basis of this choose the option he wants to follow.

If your child can't think of any solutions, you can help him by making suggestions, but you must allow him to make the decision:

"Have you thought about this -------"

"What do you think might happen if -------"

Just make a few suggestions so that your child does not become dependent on you for all the ideas.

Sometimes your child will make the right choices and things will go well. Sometimes they get it wrong and do something which is not acceptable. We as adults can help them learn from their mistakes by allowing them to face the CONSEQUENCES.

EXAMPLE

You are trying to discuss something important with your mother but your child has the television on very loud. In this situation you could shout at your child.

You: Turn off that row: Granny and I can't hear ourselves think!

Here you are telling the child to turn down the television but not giving a logical explanation why you want this, other than because you say so.

Alternatively you could try to help your child understand that the noise of the television is stopping you from doing what you want.

You: I realise that you enjoy watching that programme on the television but Granny and I are trying to talk. Either turn it down or go and play outside. The choice is yours.

Here you explain why you want the television turned down and you point out the consequence of not doing so.

EXAMPLE

John has left his toys all over the floor. This is something he does all the time and his mother is getting tired of it.

Mother: John, I have told you a thousand times to put your toys away when you have finished with them. You can forget about going to play with Tommy on Saturday.

Here the punishment is too far removed from the "crime" for the child to be able to put the two together. By Saturday, the child will not be able to remember why he can't go to play with Tommy.

Alternatively:

Mother: John, your toys are in a terrible mess again. Either tidy them up or I will put them in bags in the cellar and you will not be able to play with them for a week.

Here the consequence of not putting the toys away is very clear.

EXAMPLE

A mother is trying to get her son to bed. He is fooling about and being quite cheeky to her.

Mother: Tom, either you settle down and go into bed now or I won't read you a story. You decide.

Tom gets into bed.

Mother: That's really good. Thank you Tom. Now we can have the story.

The reason for using consequences is to encourage children to make decisions about things, not to force them into doing the things we want them to. By using consequences we allow children to make decisions about things and then to experience the consequences - good or bad. Children do eventually learn from their mistakes, although with some children it takes longer than others.

USING CONSEQUENCES TO ENCOURAGE POSITIVE BEHAVIOUR

There are several basic principles to follow when using this technique to help children behave in a positive way. You must first of all work out what is going on. What is your child doing that you don't like and what is he trying to achieve? Think about why he might be doing this. It is important when you are dealing with situations like this that you remember to treat your child with respect and start from the position that you want him to learn from the situation he is in, rather than for you to scream and shout at him because he has done something wrong which has annoyed you.

Don't over protect your child, allow him to experience the consequences of his behaviour. Don't take away the responsibility for his behaviour from him. Avoid doing for children what they can do for themselves. The more you can help them to learn to do things for themselves, the better they will feel about themselves.

Don't feel sorry for them. Pitying children tells them that they are defective in some way and that you don't think that they are capable of trying to do something for themselves. Being overprotective may help you feel better but it won't help your child.

Try to be as consistent as you can in managing misbehaviour. We can never be one hundred per cent consistent. However, it is important that we try hard to be as consistent as possible. If we are consistent, our children know what to expect. If we say we will do something then they know that we will do it. If we are inconsistent then they will not be sure what we are going to do. If children know what to expect, then they can make decisions about what to do.

Remember that it is the behaviour your child is showing that you don't like, not your child himself! It is important to show your child that you are making that distinction. Use the tone of your voice and non-verbal communication to show him that you love and respect him and it is his behaviour that you don't like.

Remember that what you are doing is important. So although family, friends and neighbours will at times disapprove of what you are doing, ignore them, allow your children to experience the consequences of their behaviour.

Does the problem belong to you or to your child? Sort out who owns it and then deal with it. (We talked about problem ownership earlier in the book.)

Remember that actions speak louder than words. Don't talk too much to your child. This can reduce the effectiveness of what you are trying to do. Children become **"parent deaf"** if you talk to them too much. When you are using consequences to help a child think about their behaviour, talk as little as possible.

Stick to what you say and do. Follow through with consequences and don't argue or fight with your child about this. Remember who is the adult. Conserve your energy. Don't get involved in long battles with your child over a point of discipline. You will end up feeling worse than your child. Once your child has made his decision about what he is going to do, let him do it and experience the consequence. Don't fight him about it or give in.

EXAMPLE

Jack wanted to go out to play on Sunday with his friend. His mother said that he could go if he behaved at the lunch table. He did not!

Jack: Mum can I go out to play now?

Mother: I'm sorry Jack but our agreement was that if you behaved at lunch you could go. You didn't behave and so you can't go out to play.

Jack: Please mum

Mother: No

Jack: Oh please mum

Mother left the room.

In this situation, Mother was very clear about what Jack would have to do if he was going to be allowed out to play with his friend. Jack did not do what was expected of him and Mother followed through with the consequence for Jack which was that he didn't get out to play. Mother avoided getting into a long battle with Jack over this by going out of the room.

When something happens involving a number of children and you didn't witness it, don't waste time and energy trying to find out who was to blame. Let all the children share the consequence, don't listen to them telling tales on each other. Letting them all share the responsibility will encourage them to work problems out amongst themselves in the future.

SUMMARY

◆ It is important to set limits for children.

◆ Help your children learn to make choices about their behaviour.

◆ Allow children to face the consequences of their choices.

◆ Don't do things for your children which they can do for themselves.

◆ Do not fight and do not give in.

TASK

1. Work out how you expect your child to behave, what the rules are and what is acceptable behaviour. Make a list of the behaviours you want and those you don't, on the **Work Sheet: Behaviour.** (you and your partner should make separate lists, then compare them and make a final list which you both agree on).

2. Practice using choices with your child. Record situations in which you use choices on the **Work Sheet: Choices.**

WORK SHEET: BEHAVIOUR

WORK SHEET: CHOICES

SITUATION   **CHOICES**

9. GIVING INSTRUCTIONS

Being able to give your child instructions effectively is an important part of behaviour management. In this section of the book we are going to discuss how to do this.

ARE INSTRUCTIONS NECESSARY?

It is important to give a child some instructions. For example, when you want them to do something, you have to tell them what it is that you want them to do. It is easy however, to use too many instructions or to use them when they are not necessary. Remember that children get **"parent deaf"** if we talk at them too much; this is especially true if we are using instructions.

EXAMPLE

A mother is watching her daughter painting.

Mother: That is a very pretty flower. I think that you should paint the petals pink and the centre yellow. You must be careful not to paint outside the lines.

The instructions this mother is giving are not really necessary. Does it really matter what colour the petals are and wouldn't it be nice for the little girl to choose?

It is important to think about the situation you are in and whether you need to give instructions. Instead of telling her daughter what to do, this mother could have simply commented on her painting. This might have led into a discussion with the little girl about the colour of flowers and where they grow.

LIMIT THE NUMBER OF INSTRUCTIONS

Sometimes we run into trouble because we give too many instructions at the same time. The child is overwhelmed. No matter how much he wants to do what you have asked he doesn't know where to start.

EXAMPLE

A little boy has been playing in the living room. His mother comes in:

Mother: Time for dinner. I want you to put all your toys away. Put the lego in the box and the cars in the garage. The computer needs to be put back in the other room. Then I want you to go upstairs and wash your hands and face. Then you can go to the dining room.

This mum uses a long list of commands that are enough to make anyone panic!

"LETS" AND "WOULD YOU LIKE TO"

"Let's tidy up" suggests to a child that you are going to help him. A problem arises if you have no intention of helping your child, but you were just saying it as a way of motivating the child to put his toys away.

"Wouldn't you like to go to bed now?" invites an answer of NO! Asking a child whether they would like to do something suggests to the child that he has a choice in the matter, which is fine if he does. If he does not however, and you are merely using this question as a way of telling him that it is time to go to bed, then you are giving him a very confusing message.

It is important that, if you want your child to do something, you tell him clearly what you want him to do. Do not offer him a choice in the matter if you do not want him to make a choice.

CLEAR INSTRUCTIONS

These are what we need to use to help children to know what is expected of them.

EXAMPLE

Mother: Sue, you must not throw your doll into the air, that is dangerous. Your doll might fall on someone and hurt them or damage the furniture.

This is a very clear instruction about not throwing dolls.

SUBSTITUTES

If you have told a child that they may not do something, it is very important that you provide a substitute for that activity, something they can do or have instead. By providing a substitute you will prevent your child from going on about what you have said they can't do.

EXAMPLE

A little boy wants to go out to play, it is raining and his mother thinks he should stay in.

Son: Can I go out to play?

Mother: I don't think that would be a good idea, it's raining. You can help me make the lunch instead.

Son: O.K.

This mother suggests that her son can cook lunch with her as a substitute for going out to play. He seems quite pleased with this and in this way mother avoids an argument about going out to play.

AVOID CRITICISM

Sometimes when we are angry we can turn instructions into criticism. Remember what we discussed earlier about the importance of conveying to your child that you love him and respect him even though you are telling him that you don't like what he is doing. Avoid criticising your child when you are telling him what to do.

EXAMPLE

A mother and her son, Simon, are sitting watching the television. Simon is fidgeting and his mother is getting angry.

Mother: Simon, for goodness sake sit still for once in your life; you are such a pest!

USING POSITIVE INSTRUCTIONS

Try to tell your children to do things in a positive way. To do this it is better to use do's rather than don'ts. Do's said in a positive, firm voice are far more effective than don'ts said with criticism and in a negative way.

ALWAYS REMEMBER TO PRAISE YOUR CHILDREN WHEN THEY HAVE DONE WHAT YOU ASKED. TELL THEM WHY YOU ARE PLEASED WITH THEM.

WHEN/THEN INSTRUCTIONS

These instructions are along the same lines as the first/then rule we discussed earlier in the book.

"**When** you have tidied up your lego, **then** you can go out to play:

Once you have used a when/then instruction it is important that you don't get into a fight about it or give in. Be consistent.

GIVE A WARNING

Sometimes it is helpful to forewarn your child that an instruction is coming. A good example is tidying up. It can be a tricky time when you suddenly announce to your child that he has to tidy up NOW! It can make it easier for a child if you warn him that he will have to tidy up soon.

"O.K. you have five more minutes before tidy up time. What would you like to do in the last five minutes."

The most important thing to remember about instructions is that they only work if you **FOLLOW THROUGH** with them. It is no good telling a child to do something if you pay no attention when he does or doesn't do as you ask. Once you have decided that you want your child to do something, it is then essential that you follow through with it.

There are several steps involved in following through with instructions which depend on the child's response. If he does as he is asked, then he should be praised immediately. If he does not follow the instruction immediately, you should repeat it and let him know that there will be a consequence for him if he does not do as you ask. He may start to whine and cry. You can prevent this by immediately distracting him onto something else. If he still does not comply then you must follow through with the consequence.

Children will try various ways to put you off from following through. They will test you out by doing things like arguing and asking "why". If this happens it is very important that you do not get involved in explaining yourself and your instruction. If you do, your child has succeeded in distracting you from following through with your instruction immediately. Children will pretend that they cannot do what you have asked in an attempt to get you to do it for them. Here it is very tempting to give in and do it yourself. It is much better to encourage the child to take the responsibility for doing what you have asked. Make sure that you follow through.

It is quite normal for children to test you out when you give an instruction to see if you really mean it, particularly if you have not been consistent in the past and have given in to them. In fact this happens quite often and so you must be prepared to have to deal with your children not doing what you ask.

EXAMPLE

A father and son have been playing with some cars. It is time to put them away.

Father: Sam it's time to tidy up. Let's put the cars away.

Sam: OK

Father: Why don't you start putting them away? Come on Sam, please put them away.

Sam: In a minute.

Father: It's almost bedtime.

Sam: No.

Father: Right, cars away and bedtime now.

Father hands Sam a car to put in the box, Sam continues to play with it.

This father makes a few mistakes. He uses let's and why don't you's. Sam ignores his father's requests to put the cars away which results in his father getting angry.

EXAMPLE

A father and daughter are playing with her dolls. The little girl is dancing around the room with the dolls.

Father: Sue, it is time to put the dolls away now. Where do they go?

Sue: In the box.

Father: Good, that's right. You put them away in the box.

Sue puts the dolls away in the box.

Father: Well done Sue, that was very good, you put all the dolls away in the box.

This father uses clear instructions to let his daughter know what she has to do. He involves her in thinking about where the dolls go and praises her as she makes a start at putting her toys away.

Children will test out rules and instructions.

EXAMPLE

A mother and her two children Simon and Steven, have been playing at the kitchen table with cars. It is time to tidy up.

Mother: O.K. boys, you have one minute to tidy up so I can start dinner.

The timer goes off one minute later.

Mother: O.K. boys, time's up.

Simon: Can't we have a bit longer mum, please. I want to finish this game.

Mother: (ignoring Simon's plea) Come on Steven, let's put the cars away. It really is time to tidy up. I have to get dinner ready.

This mum gives her children a warning that time is nearly up. There are a few problems with what she is doing however. Firstly, one minute isn't long enough for the boys to finish their games. She also misses the opportunity to reward Steven for starting to tidy up.

USING DISTRACTION

When you tell a child that they are not allowed to do something, it can sometimes be useful to distract him immediately in some way. This may have the effect of preventing him from protesting or becoming more disruptive.

EXAMPLE

A mother and her daughter are playing with crayons. The little girl tries to colour the wallpaper.

Mother: Oh, we are not supposed to draw on the wall. This is what we do with the crayons, (taking the crayons from her daughter and starting to draw a picture).

EXAMPLE

Mum is making dinner in the kitchen whilst her her son is playing with a computer game.

Mother: Time to switch the game off.

Sam: Why?

Mother: It has been on for long enough today. What other toys would you like to play with now? (coming through from the kitchen and going over to the toy box) Oh look what I have found (pulling out the hand puppets) Sam turn off the game.

Sam turns off the game and goes over to his mother and starts playing with the puppets.

In both these situations, the mother successfully used a substitute to distract her child.

DON'T ARGUE ABOUT INSTRUCTIONS

Children learn very quickly how to distract their parents from enforcing instructions. You must keep your wits about you and avoid getting into arguments with your children about rules and instructions.

AVOIDANCE TACTICS

This is another technique used by children to distract their parents from following through. They will try to get their parents involved in "why" games. If you get into a "why" game all you are doing is reinforcing your child's non-compliance.

EXAMPLE

Two girls Sarah and Gemma, have been playing on the living room floor.

Mother: It's time to tidy up.

Sarah: Ah, why?

Mother: Because it's time to go to bed. You can do just one more thing. (She notices that Gemma has done one more thing) O.K. Gemma, that was one more thing. Now tidy up. Sarah what is your last thing?

Gemma: Mum why does this horse fall over? (picking up a plastic model).

Mother: Because its leg is broken. Now put the toys away girls.

Gemma: But why is its leg broken? Can't we mend it?

Mother: Come on Gemma. Let's put the things away. Sarah, have you started to put anything away yet?

Sarah: No, I haven't done my one last thing yet.

Mother: Well hurry up then.

You can just imagine this "game" going on and on with the children asking more and more "why" questions and successfully distracting their mother from her instruction to tidy up and go to bed.

Children will try all sorts of things to distract you, whining, screaming and arguing. Don't be put off, **ignore** their attempts to distract you. Don't talk to your child or give eye contact when you are ignoring them even if they start screaming! Your child will be cross because they have not got their own way and they are testing you out to see if you really mean what you say.

The only exception to this rule of ignoring some bad behaviour is if your child is doing something destructive or harmful to another person. In this situation you should use another technique. We will discuss some of these techniques in the remaining chapters of the book.

THE IMPORTANCE OF PRAISE

As always it is extremely important to praise children as soon as they do what you have asked them to. Praising children when they have done as you asked will make it much more likely that they will do as you ask in the future.

GOODNIGHT MUM... DONT WAIT UP FOR ME!!

SUMMARY

◆ Use clear instructions.

◆ Use do's rather than don'ts.

◆ Try to give a warning that an instruction is coming.

◆ Avoid unnecessary instructions.

◆ Involve children in making house rules.

◆ Don't get into arguments about instructions.

◆ Try to divert and distract your child before he gets a chance to "not comply" with what you want him to do.

◆ Ignore inappropriate responses.

◆ Praise children immediately when they do as they are asked.

TASK

1. Try counting the number of instructions you use on any one day and record some of them on the Work Sheet: Instructions.
2. Try to reduce the number of instructions you use.
3. Practice using clear, direct and specific instructions. Avoid "let's" and "wouldn't you like to".
4. Praise your child when he does as he is asked.

WORK SHEET: INSTRUCTIONS

INSTRUCTIONS   **CHILD'S RESPONSE**

10. TIME OUT

Many of you probably already use Time Out, but as with all behaviour management techniques, there are some basic rules which, if you follow them closely, will make it more effective.

If children don't do as they are asked or told or if they do something we don't like, then sometimes we have to use sanctions such as, "If you don't stop that now then you won't be allowed to play with the cars for the rest of the day". There will always be times however, in spite of such sanctions, when children don't do as they are asked. In these situations we have to know what else we can do - what other techniques we can use. **Time Out** is something which you can use.

Time Out involves putting the child in a chair or in a boring place for a period of time, when he has done something we didn't want him to. Time out is effective in reducing problem behaviours, even in quite young children and it works because:

1. **It stops the child from carrying on with the behaviour you want to stop.**

2. **It removes him from the situation and so prevents him from getting any further attention for the behaviour.**

3. **It gives both you and your child time to cool off.**

RULES FOR USING TIME OUT

There are a few basic but important rules for using Time Out as follows:

1. Decide what behaviours you will use Time Out for.

This is a very important thing to do. Time Out will be effective for most behaviours but it is important that you don't over use it. Don't use it for every misdemeanor, but save it for the behaviours which you really can't ignore and which you want to stop immediately. Time Out should be reserved for serious behaviours such as aggression or destructiveness. You should take some time to think about what you are going to use Time Out for, before you explain it to your child.

2. Explain Time Out to your child

It is very important to explain to your child what Time Out is before using it. This should be done when you are both calm and his behaviour is reasonable. Time Out should be explained as something which you are going to use to help him on those occasions when he has got into a mess doing something which you don't like. It is important to tell your child which behaviours will result in Time Out. Keep your description brief! Don't give your child a lecture and avoid criticising him or implying that you are using Time Out because he is bad.

3. Decide where your child will go during Time Out

Where a child goes during Time Out is up to you. You must work out something which you feel comfortable with in your house. The Time Out place should ideally be somewhere that is boring and somewhere the child is not going to have fun. Some people choose to use a chair in a corner of the room or in a place where there is little going on - such as the hallway. You can arrange it so that your child is still in sight but **don't interact with him during Time Out.** Some people choose to put their child in their bedroom for Time Out. You must make sure that there are no dangerous things or places in the room first of all.

4. Decide how long Time Out will last

A rough guide is to make Time Out the same length in minutes as the child's age in years. Time Out should not be longer than 10 minutes whatever the situation. The main aim of Time Out is to stop the undesirable behaviour immediately.

Children will resist Time Out. They will scream and yell and throw things about and resist going to Time Out. In this situation you can tell your child that you are going to add another minute to the Time Out period. If they continue to resist, add in other things like removal of privileges - such as watching television or going out to play. He may also try and leave Time Out before the time is up.

You must take him back immediately and start Time Out all over again.

For very young children, the length of time is not that important. The really important thing about Time Out is that you are stopping a behaviour which you don't like. You may have to remove the child from what he is doing physically if he cannot do this for himself. You may also have to hold on to him for a while if he is very distressed and screaming and kicking etc. Stay calm and wait until he shows signs of calming down. Then try and distract him on to something else. **Do not** start to talk to him about what went wrong as this is likely to start the behaviour off again. Remember, you are in control of Time Out at all times. You decide when it is over, not your child. Most children will test you out over Time Out at first - they want to see if you really mean it. This will stop if you show your child that you really do mean it.

It is important that you try to praise your child for something positive as soon as you can after Time Out is over so try to get him involved in something that he can enjoy doing.

EXAMPLE

A mother is talking to her son about his behaviour. He has been biting his young brother.

Mother: Paul, I want to talk to you about something. I am worried about you biting Jamie. It makes me unhappy when you do that and it hurts him. I am going to try to help you to stop doing that. When you bite Jamie, you will have to sit on the chair in the hallway for 5 minutes. If you don't bite him then you won't have to sit on the chair. Do you understand?

Paul: Yes Mum.

Mother: Good. Lets see how well you can do!

This mother talks to her son about the behaviour she does not like and explains clearly to him what she is going to do to help him. She tells him when he will go for Time Out and how long it will last.

DEALING WITH A CHILD WHO REFUSES TO GO TO TIME OUT

When a child refuses to go to Time Out it is very easy to get really angry, to start yelling and shouting. This is exactly what they want - it is giving them more attention and diverting you from Time Out. Don't get angry - keep going with the Time Out and then start to add in other things like loss of privileges. Remember as always you must mean what you say and follow through.

EXAMPLE

A father has decided to use Time Out to discipline his son. His son is refusing to go.

Father: Time Out David, off you go.

David: No, I'm not going, that's just stupid.

Father: (remaining calm) That makes it 6 minutes now not 5.

David: See if I care.

Father: (calmly) That's 7 minutes.

David: I don't have to go.

Father: 8 minutes. If you don't go now then you will not be allowed to play outside until Saturday.

David: That's not fair.

Father: Forget going out to play then.

David: (starts to go to Time Out). I was just going anyway.

This father remains calm and sticks to the rules of Time Out. He remains quite neutral and does not get into a fight with his son even when he starts to be quite cheeky. David realises that his dad means what he says and eventually goes to Time Out. He may think twice about trying this again.

REMEMBER

You must mean what you say. Don't make threats and then not follow through. Your child will quickly learn that you don't mean it and will not take any notice of you.

It takes a great deal of energy to follow through all the time. Sometimes it seems as though it would be easier to just give in. That might take the pressure off right now, but it will make it ten times harder to deal with misbehaviour the next time around. Your child will think that you don't mean what you say and will keep going to see when you will give in. So find that extra bit of energy now, don't make life harder for yourself in the long run.

SUMMARY

◆ Explain Time Out when both you and your child are calm.

◆ Explain what behaviours will result in Time Out.

◆ Explain where Time Out will be and how long it will last.

◆ Take small children to Time Out. Older children can go by themselves.

◆ Don't get into a discussion about Time Out.

◆ Let your child out of Time Out as soon as he settles.

◆ Don't lecture your child once Time Out is over.

◆ Involve your child in something positive as soon as Time Out is over and praise him.

◆ Use Time Out for destructive behaviours or behaviours which you cannot ignore.

TASK

1. Decide what behaviour you are going to use Time Out for and work out how you are going to apply Time Out.

2. Explain Time Out to your child.

3. Record when you use Time Out and your child's response on the record sheet: Time Out.

WORK SHEET: TIME OUT

BEHAVIOUR   **CHILD'S RESPONSE**

11. MANAGING BEHAVIOUR OUTSIDE THE HOME

Misbehaviour when it happens outside your own home is always more difficult to manage than when it happens at home. You feel embarrassed, people are watching and often passing comments about what they would do "if he was my child". Your child seems to sense that you are in a weaker position because you are not at home and his behaviour seems much worse.

In this section of the book we are going to discuss how you can manage difficult behaviour when it happens outside your home, in the supermarket, at the park or at the cinema. Very simply, this involves using some of the techniques we have discussed already and working out how you can use them to help your child with his behaviour in public places. Before we go on to discuss this in more detail we will go over some of the techniques.

MISBEHAVIOUR AND HOW TO DEAL WITH IT

All children misbehave at times. It is therefore important to think about how you are going to deal with your child when they misbehave. The first thing to do is to work out why your child is misbehaving. At this point it might be useful to remind yourself of the reasons why children misbehave by reviewing chapter 3. It is very important that you try to be as consistent as possible when you are dealing with misbehaviour. Decide how you are going to handle it and then do it – **always** follow through.

The first thing to remember about misbehaviour is that it will not happen if your child is actively engaged in a positive activity. It is important therefore to try to anticipate your child's needs. Think ahead and try to make sure that your child has something to do throughout the day. When your child is becoming frustrated and bored try to think of something else for him to do. You can involve him in the things you are doing, housework, gardening, making the beds and so on. Children really enjoy helping their parents and in particular, they enjoy doing things with their parents. I am sure you can think of lots of routine chores you could involve your child in. The same applies when you are out somewhere with your child. Think about where you are going and what you are going to do. Think about it from your child's point of view and try to think of things he can do. Involve him in what you are going to do or find something else for him to do.

If your child does misbehave you must do something about it quickly. This is where your ground rules become important and your decisions about what is acceptable behaviour and what is not. If the misbehaviour is minor, the best thing to do is to ignore it. Remember the effect of attention on behaviour and that even negative attention such as shouting and yelling will reinforce misbehaviour and make it more likely that it will happen again. It is therefore much better to completely ignore minor misbehaviour. The secret here is to COMPLETELY IGNORE the misbehaviour – no eye contact, no physical contact and no verbal contact. Don't look at your child, walk away from your child, turn your back on him and don't say a word.

It is quite hard to completely ignore a child who is doing something you don't particularly like. Children are also quite good at trying to get adult attention. It is likely your child will increase the behaviour you are ignoring to see if he can get your attention. He may even start crying and whinging. Whilst your child might settle faster if you pay attention to him at this point he will have learned that if he keeps going long enough you will give in and he will get away with the misbehaviour. Again ignore whinging and crying but the moment it stops you must pay attention to your child once again and praise him for something positive, try to distract him on to another more positive activity. Remember the combination of ignoring and distracting works really well for minor misbehaviour – if it is used consistently.

MY JOHN LOVES COMING SHOPPING AND HE'S SO WELL BEHAVED.

For more serious misbehaviour, you have to do something to stop it immediately. Remember things like the first / then rule and the when / then rule, loss of privileges and Time Out are all things you can use to stop misbehaviour.

STAY CALM, It is really important that through all of this you stay calm. Sometimes your child's misbehaviour will really annoy you and it is hard not to yell and scream. This will not help matters, you will feel guilty about losing your temper and your child will be frightened by your outburst. Try to stay calm and handle the misbehaviour using the techniques you already know.

As always it is important to remember that whilst we are discussing ways to reduce misbehaviour, you must look out for the positive things your child does everyday and encourage those by praising and rewarding your child when he behaves well.

Remember that your child will test you out for a while to see if you are really serious about ignoring his misbehaviour and so the misbehaviour will get worse for a while before it gets better.

We are now going to take what you have learned already one step forward. You are going to start using the techniques you have learned in situations outside home as well. It is likely that you have been doing this already. That is how it should be. As the techniques we have been discussing become second nature to you, you will use them everywhere and anywhere and will even forget that what you are doing is behaviour management - it will become so natural to you to interact with your child in this new, more positive way.

So, let's start to think about behaviour management outside the home. First of all we must ask some questions about the behaviour.

WHERE DOES YOUR CHILD MISBEHAVE?

There are many settings outside the home in which parents find it hard to handle their children's misbehaviour. The supermarket usually comes up somewhere on the list, department stores, the cinema, restaurants, the bus or the train and church are some of the situations which commonly cause problems. Think about which situation you find the worst, or which you dread going to or have even started avoiding because it is so awful.

WHAT HAVE YOU TRIED IN THE PAST TO GET HIM TO BEHAVE IN THESE SITUATIONS?

Try thinking through the last incident when you were out that you found difficult. Try and run through a blow by blow account of what you and your child did and said. What things did you do to try to get him to stop misbehaving?

WHAT ARE THE ALTERNATIVES?

The first step in managing difficult behaviour outside the home is to try to avoid it or prevent it happening in the first place. Already you will be aware of the places you dread going with your child because his behaviour is usually really difficult there. If you know the places and situations which are really difficult for your child, take some time to think of ways round them. Do you have to take your child there? For example, can you go to the supermarket on your own when your child is at school or nursery, or will someone look after him for you while you go. Supermarkets are really rather boring places for children and this may be one of the reasons your child gets into difficulties there. Because it is a boring place he will try to make it more fun, by running up and down the aisles or taking things off the shelves. Also there are all those wonderful sweets and crisps and toys that he wants! Some supermarkets now have creches where you can leave your child while you do the shopping. However, it can be difficult leaving a hyperactive child in these places. If your child has to go with you, what can you do to make it an easier experience for both of you?

You are trying to prevent misbehaviour occurring in the first place. Think ahead and consider how you can make the trip to the supermarket more fun for your child. Use the techniques you have learned from this book. Which ones could you use in this situation? What about the **FIRST / THEN** rule. (Page 40)

You can use this rule to:

FIRST

1. Tell your child what is going to happen - you are going to go to the supermarket because you have to get some food.

2. Tell your child what you expect of him while you are there.

THEN

3. What he will get if he behaves in the way you have asked him to. Here you can build in some sort of reward.

Another technique you can use is to keep your child busy whilst you are at the supermarket. Get him to help you look for things on the shelf. Talk to him about the products you are buying, for example, where do eggs come from, where do we get milk from? In this way you will involve him in the activity and show him that you think he is a responsible person by asking him to help you.

To summarise

- think ahead, identify situations which might be difficult

- plan ahead; once you have identified the difficult situations, plan what you are going to do and how you are going to involve your child in the activity

- tell your child what you expect of him in the situation

- plan a reward for your child if he behaves as you have asked and tell him what the reward will be.

Don't forget to give your child lots of praise when he behaves well in situations. By praising behaviour as soon as it has happened you will encourage it to happen again.

So if you think ahead about situations you know are difficult or new situations which might be difficult, you can try to plan the activity in such a way that your child knows what is expected of him. Keep him involved and busy throughout the activity and praise and reward him when he does what you have asked.

Another useful technique is to praise a child who is behaving well and ignore the one who is misbehaving. In this way you are using the child who is behaving well as a model. The misbehaving child will try to behave in order to get praise like the other child. It is important, however, not to overdo this and to find a way to praise the child who was misbehaving as soon as possible.

Remember to praise even the smallest positive things your child does.

It is really **hard not to get angry** sometimes when your child is being aggressive, difficult, defiant or is constantly whining. Sometimes it feels as though your child is doing it on purpose just to get at you. Try to avoid thinking of your child's behaviour as a personal attack on you. It is not. **STAY CALM.** Don't show your anger or distress. Remember that it is your child's misbehaviour that you don't like and not him. What you want to do is to stop the behaviour. It can be quite frightening for a child to be confronted by an angry adult who is in charge but who looks as though they might go out of control any time! Remember what you are doing; you want to respond to the behaviour in a way which will make it much less likely that it will happen again.

We will now go on to look at some examples of what we have been discussing.

AVOIDING MISBEHAVIOUR

Sometimes we can avoid misbehaviour.

EXAMPLE

A mother and her daughter Susie aged 5 are visiting mother's friend who has an 18 month old daughter called Jane. Susie is playing with some toys when Jane grabs one.

Susie: (screams) Hey you. That's mine. Give it here. (she goes to hit Jane).

Mother: (moves in and picks up Jane and gives the toy back to Susie). Come on Jane let's go and look what's over here - Oh look it's your Postman Pat book. Isn't that nice? Shall we look at it for a while? (Susie has resumed her game).

Here the mother is very effective in removing the younger child and stopping her interfering with the older child's play. She stops the younger child from getting frustrated by immediately distracting her onto something else.

It would in fact be very hard for these two children to play together without falling out. Children of 18 months have little idea about sharing and the 5 year old will be too serious about her game to want to involve the little girl. The mother does the right thing here. She separates them and gets them involved in separate activities. She senses that the little girl will be upset at not being allowed to play with Susie's toys and so she distracts her onto something else.

EXAMPLE

A father and son are playing with some tools and some nuts on the wheel of a toy car. The little boy is trying to tighten the screw.

Father: That is really tricky isn't it? It is hard to get hold of it properly. Can I help?

Son: No.

Father: (notices that the screw will not tighten unless the nut on the other side is held tight). Tell you what, if I hold the car that will mean that you have both hands free and you can hold the screw driver on one side and the spanner on the other, then the nut won't move and the screw will tighten. Well done!

This little boy is attempting to do something which is quite difficult. His father notices that he is struggling and getting frustrated. He offers to help but his son rejects this at first. He is determined to do it for himself. Father then thinks of a way of helping which does not mean doing it all for his son. He is enthusiastic and encourages and praises his son.

IGNORE MISBEHAVIOUR AND DISTRACT ONTO SOMETHING ELSE

Sometimes it is better to ignore misbehaviour altogether. Remember that children's misbehaviour is maintained by the attention they are given for the behaviour. Even nagging and screaming is a form of giving attention! If you ignore behaviour there is no reward at all. If at the same time as ignoring misbehaviour, you reward good behaviour, then the child will learn that it is better to behave because then you get some attention.

EXAMPLE

Adam who is three years old and his mother are in an electrical shop. Adam wants to play with one of the video recorders.

Mother: No Adam, the video is not for playing with. You can look at it but you must not play with it. Here, I've got one of your cars with me. Shall we play with it? (Adam continues to show interest in the video). We are not going to play with the video. (Adam begins to scream and whine). No you are not allowed to play with the video. Do you want to play with the car? (Adam stands looking at the video - finally mother moves in and picks Adam up and moves him away from the video and sits him on the floor on the other side of the shop. He starts to scream.

Mother responds by turning away from him, avoids looking at him and does not say anything to him. He stops screaming).

Adam: Will you play cars with me?

Mother tells Adam that he cannot play with the the video and then attempts to distract her son onto something else. This does not work and eventually the mother decides to physically remove her son from the video. He protests very loudly against this. She ignores this and avoids reinforcing it.

It would be important for this mother to go on to reward her son for playing with the car.

84

THINGS TO AVOID

Avoid giving attention for misbehaviour!

EXAMPLE

Jenny and her older sister Sarah are at a coffee morning with their mother who is running thecreche. Jenny is crying because her mother has taken her away from the painting she and her sister Sarah were doing.

Mother: Jenny you deliberately splashed paint on the wall. Come here. So I'm sorry but you cannot play with the paints any more.

Jenny: (crying loudly) I won't do it again.

Mother: (lifts her onto her lap and hugs and rocks her). Well I'm sorry Jenny but you can't play with the paints at the moment. Perhaps you can play with them again later. (Mum continues to hug the little girl as she screams and cries).

Here the mother is giving attention for the misbehaviour. She is giving physical comfort and is even saying sorry for stopping the misbehaviour. She is also failing to praise Sarah who is playing properly with the paints and so missed the chance of using Sarah as a model for the behaviour she would like to see from Jenny.

SUMMARY

◆ Anticipate behaviour problems. Think ahead and use past experience to imagine what might happen.

◆ Plan ahead. Before you go out think how you can deal with the problems which might arise.

◆ Decide how you want your child to behave. Don't set your goals too high - you may have to work up to the desired behaviour in steps.

◆ Work out what reward you will give if your child behaves as you want.

◆ Work out what the consequence will be if he does not behave as you ask.

◆ Always follow through!

TASK

1. Keep working on the behaviours you want to reduce and the ones you want to encourage.

2. Over the next week, on the Work Sheet: Praise and Ignore, write down the behaviours you praised, the ones you ignored and your child's response.

3. Think of a situation in public which has been difficult in the past. Use the plan described above to work out a way to manage your child's behaviour in that situation. Practice this a couple of times over the next week.

4. Keep up with your special play time with your child.

WORK SHEET: PRAISE AND IGNORE

BEHAVIOUR PRAISED	BEHAVIOUR IGNORED	CHILD'S RESPONSE

12. THE FUTURE

Now that we are coming to the end of the book, it would be a good idea to review all the things that have been discussed so far. Check out how many of the techniques you are using and how they are working. If they are not working think about why this might be and what you can do to make it more likely that they will work.

It is very important that you continue to use all the techniques you have learned. Remember that the problems won't go away overnight so you have to keep working at them. You must be determined that you are going to help your child with his problems. The work you do now to help him will make life so much better for him and for yourself in the future. Although it seems as though you are having to do all the work right now, your child will learn from what you are doing and will eventually learn to control his own behaviour.

It is very easy to slip and to give up. It is particularly easy to slip when things seem to have gone backwards and your child's behaviour seems to have got worse again. You feel like there is no point in going on. It is very important when this happens that you don't give up! Your child's success depends on your keeping going. Check up on yourself every now and again to see if you are still using the techniques you have learned and if you are using them properly.

In this section we are going to think about how to deal with problems which may arise in the future. Who knows what they will be, but undoubtedly there will be problems. It may be that your child starts showing problems that he had in the past, problems that you thought you had got over. Don't panic when this happens, just go back to what you did before in order to stop the problem and use those techniques all over again. If it is a completely new problem, then you have to stop and think about it for a while and decide what it is about and how you can most easily stop it. Is it a behaviour which you can ignore or is it something which you feel you have to stop straight away? Think about all the techniques you have learned and decide which you think you can best use.

Remember that if you and your child are doing something fun together then there is much less chance of his misbehaving. Try and increase the amount of time you and your family spend playing and doing nice things with your child. His behaviour will demand a lot of attention from you until he has learned how to control it, so in the meantime, try making as much of the attention you give him about doing fun things together.

At times it is hard to like your child. You get demoralised by his behaviour and feel as though you are a failure as a parent. You are not a failure. When you feel like this try to remember that you are doing a very good job of bringing up a child who has extremely difficult behaviour problems.

When you feel as though you don't like your child any more and you can't stand the sight of him, try to remember that it is not him that you don't like. What you don't like is the fact that he is hyperactive. Separate your child as a person from his behaviour disorder.

MYSTIC MUM

MANAGING FUTURE BEHAVIOUR PROBLEMS

Hopefully the future for you and your child will be bright, your child will lead a full and successful life and you will enjoy watching him grow. Using the techniques we have discussed so far in this book, you will be in a stronger position to help your child learn to control his behaviour.

It would however be unrealistic to suppose that your child will never present any behaviour problems again in the future. We know that the behaviour of hyperactive children changes as they get older, although exactly what changes and how, varies from child to child. In general, children become less hyperactive as they get older, they are better able to sit down, to walk instead of run and may even be less fidgety. In many cases however, children do continue to have problems attending and concentrating and in controlling their impulsivity. Their problems with relationships with other people also tend to persist, although, with time, some children do get better at making and keeping friends.

So, it is likely that your child will present you with some problems in the future. It is important that you are prepared for these. If you are prepared it is much more likely that you will be able to help your child with his problems and achieve a successful outcome for him and you. If you are not prepared, there is a risk that both you and your child will get in a mess.

So what are these problems likely to be? There may be more of the same problems that you are dealing with now, some of the problems you dealt with in the past may come back and it is very probable that new problems will emerge as your child gets older and faces new challenges and situations. You know what to do about old problems and those you are dealing with now – you must continue to use the techniques you have used before which you know work. Remember the most effective way to get rid of a behaviour you don't like is to ignore it completely. Combine ignoring with distracting onto a positive activity. The combination of ignoring and distracting is very powerful in stopping misbehaviour. If you really cannot ignore the misbehaviour because it is aggressive or destructive then do something to stop the behaviour very quickly. Remove your child from the situation by using TIME OUT. You can use all of these techniques for new problems your child presents. You can make use of star charts to encourage appropriate behaviour and loss of privileges if children do not comply with your requests for appropriate behaviour.

Remember the importance of house rules. You will have to revise house rules, abandon some and make new ones as children get older. It is important to remember to involve older children in negotiations about house rules. It is much more likely that a child will comply with a rule if they feel that they have had some say. However, it is important to remember who is in control when you are negotiating.

Our aim in all of this work is to help your children learn to control their own behaviour. As we have already discussed children learn about behaviour control in different ways. At first, very young children are totally dependent on their parents to control their behaviour, as they get older they start to take some control for themselves. This self-control gradually develops over the years until we are totally responsible for our own behaviour. The rate at which this self control develops varies from child to child, some achieve it faster than others. Because of their problems hyperactive children tend to find this process more difficult, take longer to achieve it and need more help.

You can help your child with this process by using all the techniques you have learned so far and some more which we are going to discuss now.

One of ways in which children learn is through watching what other people do, their parents, their teachers, other adults and their peers. For young children, their parents are undoubtedly the most important people in this learning process. By modelling appropriate behaviour and the sort of behaviour you wish to see from your child, you can help him learn what is acceptable and what is not. So, try to show your child by how you act and behave what you would like him to do.

ATTENTION AND CONCENTRATION

As I mentioned above, your child may continue to have problems concentrating on things. This may cause difficulties for him at home, at school and socially. You can use many of the things we have talked about already to help with this but you must develop the techniques as your child gets older.

"Special play" time provides a useful opportunity to work on your child's attention and concentration. You can help your child maintain his attention and interest on a toy or game by playing with him. When you see that he is beginning to lose interest, think of some way to bring his attention back. Help him to think of new things that he can do with his toy cars and garage or further things to draw and paint. Help him to use his imagination by showing him how you use yours.

Many hyperactive children have problems with day-to-day tasks like getting up and getting dressed. You get them out of bed in the morning and tell them to wash and put on their clothes (when they are old enough to do this for themselves). When you go back five minutes later to see how they are getting on, they have got distracted and are doing something else. Remember what we discussed earlier about using instructions (Chapter 9). It is very important not to use too many instructions at the same time. **Break day-to-day tasks into small chunks** to give your child a chance to remember what he is supposed to be doing. When you get him up in the morning, take him to the bathroom and once he has finished that task, give him the next one to do.

Teachers have to use this technique for hyperactive children in the school setting. Hyperactive children often find it hard to cope when they are given a long list of work tasks to do. Teachers have to break the tasks down into manageable bits and often give the child a break to play for a few minutes in between. In this way a child can work through the tasks, finish things and be pleased with his success, rather than be demoralised because he never finishes what he has been asked to do.

IMPULSIVITY

Hyperactive children often continue to have problems with impulse control. They rush in without thinking about the consequences of their behaviour. In chapter 8 we talked about ways in which you can help your child to learn to think through the consequences of their behaviour, by helping them to think about the choices they have in the way they behave. Help your child to stop and think about situations and then chose how they want to behave. The important part of this technique is allowing your child to live with the consequences of their choices. If they make the correct choice you must praise them. **Immediate praise** will encourage your child to behave in the same way again. If your child makes the wrong choice, perhaps choosing to behave in a way that is unacceptable to you, you must **follow through** with the consequence of that choice. Always try to allow your child to have another go at getting it right another day.

PROBLEM SOLVING AND RELATIONSHIPS

As children get older the behaviour we expect of them becomes more complicated. This is particularly true when they start to play with other children and to form relationships with other people. Hyperactive children find making and keeping friends particularly difficult. Other people find their hyperactive and impulsive behaviour off-putting. Hyperactive children often get into conflict with other children because they have pushed to the front of the queue or taken someone's turn. When young children fall out they often resort to pushing and fighting, yelling and shouting at each other as a way of solving things. This frequently results in tears. We can help children learn more appropriate ways of resolving conflict by modelling this for them in our own relationships and also by talking them through the situations they find themselves in.

The techniques described in chapter 8 can be developed to help children think through problems that arise in their relationships with other children.

When your child gets in a mess he will most likely come running to you. You will know by the look on his face or because he is in tears or in a bad mood that something has gone wrong. Help him go through what has happened and work out a way to solve the problem or at least learn how to manage it next time it happens. First of all you must find out what has happened. It is important to do this in a non-judgemental way.

You look really upset, do you want to tell me what has happened?

Is much more useful to your child and likely to result in him telling you what went wrong rather than:

Oh not again, why do you always have to get into trouble!

Once your child has told you what happened, you should praise him for any positive attempts he has made to solve the situation. You must then help him to think through other things that he might have done to resolve the situation. It is important to do this in a way that does not criticise or blame him. Try to help your child to think about how the other child or children involved might have been feeling.

An important part of helping your child to learn about problem solving is to help them learn how to tell other people how they feel. You have been modelling this for your child by telling him how you feel, and in particular, how his behaviour makes you feel. Help him use this technique to let other people know when they have upset him rather than using his fists!

You make me really angry when you take my toys.

Is better than a punch in the nose!

Dressing up, toys, story books and puppets can all be used to help children learn about their own and other people's feelings and how to make and keep friends. When you dress up and pretend to be someone else, you can imagine how that person might behave and how they might feel. You can use this to help your children think about how other people feel. Similarly you can use hand puppets to act out problem situations your child gets into and help him see how his behaviour makes other people feel. Again it is very important to do this in a non-critical, non-judgemental way.

There are lots of great books for children many of which help children think about how people feel and how the way we behave has an effect on other people. Most children enjoy being read to and as they get older, reading to their parents or themselves. You probably have a library somewhere nearby which you and your child can join and borrow books from. You could also have a look in the bookshop next time you are in town.

EXAMPLE

A mother and her son are playing with the hand puppets, a badger and a rabbit. The mother has the badger and the little boy has the rabbit.

Son: The rabbit has to have his lunch first because he is the best and he always gets to go first.

Mother: Oh, poor badger, that makes him feel really sad, he would like to have his lunch at the same time as rabbit, after all he and rabbit are friends.

Son: O.K., rabbit will share his lunch with badger, then they can go out to play after lunch.

Mother: That's a really nice idea. Badger is so happy that rabbit is going to play with him after lunch.

This mother is making good use of the hand puppets to help her child to think about how other people feel. I am sure that you can imagine other problems you could act out with hand puppets or toys.

I WISH SHE WOULD USE GLOVE PUPPETS LIKE EVERYONE ELSE!

AND THE RABBIT CAME IN AND SAW WHAT WAS HAPPENING —(COME ON DAD! YOU COME IN NOW !!)

SUMMARY

◆ Use the techniques you have learned so far to deal with new problems as they arise:

> Set clear rules
> Ignore misbehaviour and distract on to something positive
> Star Charts
> Time Out
> Loss of privileges
> Following through

◆ Praise positive behaviour as soon as it happens.

◆ Help your child to think about the effect of his behaviour on other people, making use of toys, books, puppets and dressing up.

TASK

1. Choose a problem to discuss with your child in the way described.
   Record what happens on the Work Sheet: Problem Solving.

2. Try and think of a game you can play with your child to help him with a problem situation or behaviour.

WORK SHEET: PROBLEM SOLVING

PROBLEM   **CHILD'S RESPONSE**

13. LOOKING AFTER YOURSELF

This chapter should have come at the beginning of the book. It is very important when you are dealing every day with a child who has got a problem, that you make sure that you look after yourself as well. You cannot expect to be able to keep going all the time and to get everything right for your child if you don't take some time to **be good to yourself.** Think of it as re-fuelling or building up energy reserves, or simply recovery time! You cannot keep giving of yourself if you don't put something back in.

Many people think that they should keep going all the time and that it is a sign of weakness to recognise that they get tired sometimes and would like to have a break. It is not a sign of weakness, it is a sign of strength. Recognising that you are a human being and that you need things as well, shows that you are a sensitive person who is aware of when you are functioning well and when you are not.

Many people are not good at being nice to themselves and so they don't bother. This gets worse when they are struggling with something, like a child with behaviour problems. They feel as though they don't deserve anything nice because they blame themselves for the way their child behaves.

If you feel like this it is very important that you do something nice for yourself, or allow someone else to do something nice for you. This will re-charge your batteries and give you the energy you need to carry on.

Take some time to think about nice "caring" things which you can do for yourself or someone can do for you. Make a list and try and do at least one of these things each day. The things should be:

*   Something nice

*   Something which is just for you

*   Something Small - smaller things are easier to manage and so are more likely to happen.

The sorts of things to think about are:

*   Having a bubble bath
*   Reading a nice magazine
*   Having a massage
*   Arranging a baby sitter and going out somewhere.

The list is endless once you get going. The list will depend on you - after all it is a list of things that you want to do.

SELF-CONTROL

It is hard sometimes to remain calm and to keep your cool, especially if your child has done something to really annoy you. All of us lose our tempers on occasions. If you have a child with behaviour problems you are particularly at risk of this. It is likely that every day and often several times each day, your child will do something you find exasperating. This builds up until you lose control and shout and yell at your child. You may well say something you later regret and undoubtedly you will feel guilty about what you have said and done.

All in all this is not useful for anyone concerned. Your blood pressure will have gone through the roof, your head will probably be pounding and you will feel as though you are ready to explode. Your child will be surprised and even frightened by your behaviour. It can be quite terrifying for young children to see their parents losing control, after all it is the grown-ups who are supposed to be looking after them and what will they do if the grown-ups can't control things? It is therefore very important to try to remain calm. This will help you to deal with the situation more effectively and will be a much better learning experience for your child. Remember that children learn about behaviour through watching how adults deal with situations. Try to model good ways of managing problems for your child.

There are a number of things you can do when you feel as though you are going to lose control. I should point out here that I am not suggesting that you should never get cross with your child. Sometimes when a child has done something very wrong or dangerous it is appropriate to tell him off and let him know that his behaviour has made you angry. This should be done immediately and quickly – short and to the point. Also it should be done in a non-critical way. You can tell your child that you are cross with him without criticising him or making him feel small and stupid.

It is important however that you do not lose control in front of your child and yell and scream. When you feel yourself beginning to get wound up you should stop and think about what is happening. Take two steps back from the situation and ask yourself the following questions. What exactly are you feeling? Are you all tensed up? What is going on to make you feel so angry? What can you do to make things better? It may be that you can walk away from the situation, ignore what your child is doing and get some time out for yourself. It may be however that your child is doing something which you have to stop immediately, in which case think about which techniques you can use to achieve this.

Through all of this try to stay calm, also try to think positively about what is going on. There is a link between how we feel and how we behave. If you think negatively about something then it is likely that you will behave in a negative way. If you think that your child is deliberately trying to wind you up and that he is a bad person you will show him that you dislike him in the way that you respond to him. On the other hand if you try to understand what is going wrong and think about a positive solution to the problem, then you are much more likely to convey to your child that whilst you don't like what he is doing, you still love and respect him.

SUMMARY

◆ Try to do something nice for yourself every day.

◆ Try to stay calm.

◆ Think positively.

TASK

1. Choose a situation over the next week in which you loose control. Try to think back over what happened once it is over. Think about the negative thoughts you had and write these down, then try to think of positive thoughts to replace these.

2. Make a list of "caring" things to do for yourself or for someone else to do for you and do at least one a day. Record what you do.

WORK SHEET: TALKING MYSELF THROUGH DIFFICULT SITUATIONS

PROBLEM SITUATION	NEGATIVE THOUGHTS	POSITIVE THOUGHTS	
			✔
			✔
			✔
			✔
			✔
			✔
			✔
			✔
			✔
			✔
			✔
			✔
			✔

NICE THINGS FOR ME

DAY   **ACTIVITY**

14. REVIEW

In working through this book, you have invested your time and energy to try to change things for the better for you and your child. You will have been introduced to some new ideas about helping your child with his behaviour problems and have been reminded of some techniques you already use.

At times you will have felt as though all your hard work was not making any difference, your child's behaviour was just the same, at times even worse and you will have felt that it is not worth the effort. At other times you will have seen some change for the better, even if only slight and this will have made it all seem worthwhile.

In summing up, at the end of the book it is useful to review some of the things we have covered. Firstly, remember what hyperactivity is all about. It is a behaviour disorder. It can be **persistent** which means, in some cases that it doesn't go away. It seems to be **inconsistent;** at times your child will apparently be able to behave and at others, he seems to be out of control. This is one of the aspects of the disorder which makes it so frustrating. If he can behave some of the time why can't he do it all the time?

The three main features of hyperactivity disorders are: **Inattention, excessive activity and impulsivity.** All children show these behaviours at times, but children with hyperactivity disorders show them in an extreme form. Remember that your child has a problem. and this is why his behaviour can be so difficult. It is this that you don't like. **You hate the fact that your child suffers from hyperactivity - you don't hate him.**

This book has described strategies for you to use to help your child with his behaviour problems, so that they will cause both him and you and your family less trouble and so that you will spend less time shouting at him and more time enjoying yourselves together, having fun. **You must keep going with all the new things you have learned** and sometimes modify them to fit new problems which will undoubtedly arise. It is important that you keep going. If you do, then your child will benefit from this. He will learn from what you are doing and will use what he learns from you to control his own behaviour. Think of the work you are doing now as an investment for the future. You want your child to succeed and be happy and what you are doing now will help to achieve those things. Eventually you will use the techniques we have discussed easily and naturally.

The techniques and strategies you have learned are a starting point for you to develop a new way of being with your child, so that you enjoy your child rather than feel constantly wound-up by his behaviour. Your child will know when you don't like him very much. Hyperactive children struggle with their **self-esteem.** They need to be reminded that we do care about them, like them and love them. Of all the things we have done, **"Special Play Time"** with your child is one of the most important,. Giving your child your undivided attention for some time during the day and having fun with him is so important. Don't miss any opportunities to do nice things with your child, to play with him and praise and encourage him. **Focus on the positive things your child does.**

Ignore misbehaviour if at all possible. That means ignoring it completely. Don't half ignore things. Half ignoring means half giving attention and attention is what keeps a behaviour going. When you can't ignore misbehaviour, do something about it quickly and effectively. Stop it immediately and with as little fuss as possible. Tell your child what is going on and remind him that he will have a chance to get it right another time. This way you are ending on a **positive** note. You are telling him that all is not lost and that he can try again.

Read over the book as often as you can until you feel as though you have really got it. Get your husband, partner, mother etc. to read it as well. Consistency is vital. You must try to respond to your child in the same way all the time. Also your partner, wife etc. must do the same as you. **Grown-ups must deal with hyperactive children consistently.** They must do and say the same thing.

Finally, remember to look after yourself. You need time to yourself to gather your strength so that you can keep going. Treat yourself in some way every day. Better still get someone else to do something nice for you. Make sure you get time off regularly. That way you have something to look forward to and you will come back from time off refreshed and ready to go again.

Never underestimate your skill as a parent. You are doing an extremely important job, raising a child with difficult problems. Believe in yourself and have confidence in what you are doing.